GROW HAIR
And
STOP HAIR LOSS

A Natural, Whole-body Approach

RESTORE YOUR HAIR FROM PEACH FUZZ TO A FULL CROWN OF GLORY

By Riquette Hofstein
Author of *Grow Hair in 12 Weeks*

Grow Hair and Stop Hair Loss
by Riquette Hofstein

Published by: Riquette International
269 S. Beverly Drive, Suite 200
Beverly Hills, CA 90212 323-654-3136

Website: www.Riquette.com

Library of Congress Control Number: 2003090761

ISBN: 0-9715088-0-1

Printed in the United States of America
0 9 8 7 6 5 4 3 2 1

Author's Note
All plants, like all medicines, may be dangerous if used improperly. If they are taken internally when prescribed for external use, or if they are taken in excess or over too long a time, allergic reactions and unpredictable sensitivities may develop.

To determine whether you are allergic to any of the recipes in this book, test preparations on a small patch of skin before using them on the hair, scalp or face.

Every effort has been made to ensure that the recipes and substances used in this book are safe when used as directed.

Keep herbs fresh and conditions of use as sterile as possible.

Dedication

To my parents, Jacques and Sarah Hofstein on their 60th wedding anniversary. For their total love and understanding, allowing me to grow and discover who I really am, without question and with total trust.

Acknowledgments

Thank you to David Letterman, Regis Philbin, Maury Povich, my webmaster Bart Smith, friends, clients, the press, the numerous TV and radio shows and the everlasting knowledge of my professors who have supported and inspired me since my days studying health and nutrition. May all your dreams transpire, your hearts embrace and your hair grow.

Table Of Contents

By Way of Introduction

Face-to-Face

with Riquette

M y goals for this book are threefold: to Educate, Motivate, and Stimulate your mind in a subject I am fiercely passionate about, hair care. I fully realize that a book is merely a tool, but books have been known to make big changes in the people who read them from time to time. I would like for you to think of this book as one of those life-altering experiences that very well could change your life. Literally.

I have been licensed in the field of tricology (the study of hair and root) for over thirty years. I opened my first clinic in 1969 in Sydney, Australia, and eventually started my company Riquette International after moving to Beverly Hills in 1982. I have seen and helped thousands of clients who come to me from all walks of life. Some of them are movie stars, rock stars, politicians, executives in Fortune 500 corporations, and others range from across the socio-economic spectrum to children, and single mothers working at the convenience store around the corner. Many of them walk through my doors as a last ditch effort, acting out of fear and desperation over the loss of, or severe damage to, their hair. Their stories are often sad and poignant cases, replete with shame, anger, and shattered self-esteem.

The information presented within these pages is derived from the very same techniques and methods I have employed to successfully—some would say, miraculously—turn the proverbial ship around and help my clients. The results have been astonishing. I have files and files of heartfelt letters of gratitude from my clients, thanking me for accomplishing what they all firmly believed was an absolute impossibility.

Since opening that little shop in Rose Bay Sydney back in 1969, my business has blossomed beyond my wildest dreams. My reputation for helping people has grown to world-renowned status. I have appeared on countless radio shows, and been published in hundreds of newspapers and magazines (*Harper's Bazaar, Vogue, Entrepreneur, Allure, Weight Watchers, People, The National Examiner,* and even *Beverly Hills, 90210—The Official Magazine* to name a few). I have appeared repeatedly on such television shows as *The Tonight Show* with Johnny Carson and *Late Night with David Letterman.* And, I've been a guest on *CNN, Live with Regis & Kathie Lee, Sally Jessy Raphael, The Maury Povich Show, Body By Jake, CBS This Morning, Hour Magazine,* and even had some fun with Don Rickles on *The Merv Griffin Show.* I've traveled throughout North America, Europe, the Far East, and Australia, speaking on what seems like just about every television and radio program that's ever been produced. I have given lectures for countless corporations and organizations, such as United Airlines, General Motors, Christian Dior, The American Cancer Society, Saks Fifth Avenue, governmental agencies, and hospitals. To top this all off, I've even been fortunate to have authored not one, but two international bestsellers, *Kitchen Cosmetics* and *Grow Hair in 12 Weeks.*

I mention all of this, not so much to impress you by doing a little name dropping, but to indicate something of just how far my passion has taken me. My penchant for helping others has reached millions around the globe. There is something behind my passion that I don't seem to get enough opportunities to speak about, and which I am convinced fuels the success of Riquette International: I really have a lot of compassion for the people who come through my doors. I completely identify with their deep-set anguish and injured dignity. Really.

I've been there. I know what it's like.

I was born in Cairo, Egypt to my very sweet and dear parents, Jacques and Sarah Hofstein. By the time we moved to Paris when I was eight, I already knew what I wanted to do. There was a hair styling academy not too far from our home. My parents, who were always encouraging my sister Paulette and I to try new things, easily agreed to allow me to go and hang around the academy. I met the headmaster and talked him into letting me run errands for the instructors. I have no idea what he thought of this precocious little girl who was so eager to work for no money, but he let me stay and listen to the lectures in exchange for the errands. And, listen I did.

When my parents moved our family to Sydney, I immediately enrolled into a four-year apprenticeship at Alexander of Alexander International Hairdressers. I was fourteen, and still in school. My parents were extremely supportive. Mummy would pick me up from school every day and cart me off to Alexander, then wait for me until I was finished. At night, she would be my model, allowing me to cut, perm, color, and do just about anything you could imagine. Papa even got into the act by allowing me to practice scalp massages and rolling curlers in his wavy, silky black hair.

After receiving my BA from the Beauty Technical College in Sydney, I avidly continued my education by studying at the Schwarzkopf Institute of Hair Research in Munich, London's Max Factor Makeup School, the International College of Aesthetics in Rome, Geneva's famous skincare institute La Prairie, and earned my certification in tricology from the prestigious René Furterer Institute in Paris. Eventually, I received advanced degrees and certifications in makeup, hair and skin care, hypnosis, and stress management in over fourteen European countries and North America.

My studies were as much an academic endeavor, as they were a personal journey for answers. During my teenage years I was afflicted with a terrible and emotionally debilitating case of acne. At times, it was so awful that I believed that all anyone could see on my face was my eyes. To make matters worse, my hair became so brittle and fragile, that it began to fall out. My parents took me to a series of doctors, and I consulted every dermatologist I could find. No one had the answer to healing my condition.

Finally, I made the realization that, if anyone was going to figure this out, then it would probably have to be me. I had to learn to trust myself, and take all my advanced training to a heretofore-unexplored territory. I began experimenting with altering my diet, taking vitamin supplements, and using herbs. This was back in the days when the field of herbology was still very new, and still regarded with a great deal of skepticism. If anything, my travels throughout the world brought me in direct contact with a lot of stories and folklore about the use of herbs in curing the body of ailments. I tried them all, in every combination I could think of. Eventually, I did find the answer. My skin cleared up, and my hair became more lush, beautiful, and healthy than ever before.

Then, I made an intuitive leap that changed my life: If it worked for me, surely it'll work for someone else. A lucid understanding of my greater purpose, meaning, and connection for my life washed over me. I had found my passion: to Educate, Motivate, and Stimulate other people toward their optimal beauty, vitality, and health.

This book represents a major step toward the fulfillment of that life purpose. Some people who may have either read, or heard of, my last book, *Grow Hair in 12 Weeks*, may be wondering, "Why the need for a second book?" The answer lies in a lot of questions that came from my clients after the first one was published. They would say something like, "I read your book, Riquette, and I really loved it, but… How come you didn't say anything about your diet?" Or, "How come you didn't include a section about hypnosis?" And, "What's the difference between a tincture and a decoction?"

Not being the kind of person to ignore such a loud and clear message, I eventually got around to putting those other things on paper, and here they are. Of course, if anyone finds that I missed something else, please let me know.

First Impressions

Hair's Intimate Connection to Our Personal Identities

In the summer of 1991, high in the Tyrolean Alps of Northern Italy, a team of archeologists and other scientists retrieved the preserved body of a man buried in the glacial fields. First impressions led the body's discoverers to assess that he was a hiker who had been caught in an avalanche, and had perhaps only been dead for four or five decades at most. Upon closer inspection of his clothes and tools, the team adjusted the estimate of his date of death to almost 5,300 years before!

What was the thing that gave the appearance that this Neolithic mummy, now known as the Iceman, to have been an inhabitant of the Twentieth Century? In short, it was his hair—the manner in which it was cut, and the fact that his beard was trimmed to boot.

The Iceman has revealed much about life at the dawn of the Copper Age, including the fact that our modern concern with appearances, particularly when it comes to hair, is not by any means a new sociological development. Indeed, a cursory examination of civilization throughout the ages will show that hair, how it appears and how styles have evolved, has always been an important part of our development as a species.

The way we wear our hair is closely tied to the times we live in, and to the society into which we are born. As new hairstyles develop and emerge, you can be certain that substantial cultural changes are taking place.

Remember when Farah Fawcett rose to stardom with her feathered mane and virtually every woman in Western civilization raced to her hairdresser? What else was going on in society, but the Sexual Revolution? Remember when Demi Moore emerged as a superstar in Ghost? After that movie's opening weekend, every woman in America started asking for the same cut Demi had. Women were just beginning to make their mark as independent spirits climbing the ladder of a booming corporate economy. And, when Bruce Willis debuted with his buzz-cut opposite Cybill Shephard in Moonlighting, while Don Johnson worked the streets with a stubble beard in Miami Vice, America turned toward massive consumerism and junk bonds during the Reagan Years. That was quickly followed by radical hairstyles from Cyndi Lauper, Madonna, and Flock of Seagulls as a sort of anti-establishment answer to what was going on in the mainstream.

Rock musicians and movie stars have, of course, not always been the purveyors of fashion when it comes to how we wear our hair. Politicians, aristocrats, and religious leaders throughout the centuries have had a profound influence on the culture of hair. From the Pharaohs of Egypt, to the first Caesar of Rome, to the monks of the Middle Ages, and Louis the XIV (who adopted the fashion of wearing powdered wigs to cover his balding crown), hair has always held a close tie to the evolution of world society.

When Samson, a man of apparently insuperable strength and power, fell in love with the Philistine Delilah, we are told that his head was adorned with seven long braids, having been forbidden by God from ever submitting to a haircut. Delilah was charged by Samson's copious enemies with the duty of discerning the key to his downfall. After several failed attempts, she beguiled him into revealing his secret: "There hath not come a razor upon mine head," he said, "for I have been a Nazarite unto God from my mother's womb: if I be shaven, then my strength will go from me, and I shall become weak, and be like any other man." (Judges 16:17, KJV)

Not long after that, Samson was arrested, given a haircut, and, in an apocalyptic catastrophe, was killed along with his Philistine enemies.

Clearly this allegory was not intended to be a warning from God against hair loss, but many men today can relate to the visceral fear of the toll that androgenetic alopecia (genetic balding) can have on their virility.

If anything, the story of Samson, and the collective anxiety that men and women share of going bald, illustrates how closely our hair is tied to our personal identities. Our hair, or lack thereof, is presumed, albeit unconsciously, to be a direct reflection of our personalities, our confidence, our sexual identities, and our outlook on life. Unfortunately, with today's emphasis on giving a good first impression in the job market and in the new realm of the online dating scene, this assumption has only gained in paramount importance.

Go to your favorite Internet search engine and type in the word "hair." The results will undoubtedly number in the tens of thousands, with the range of topics covering everything you can imagine: Chinese medicinal practices, how to find a good hair salon, conspiracy theories on the false cancer warnings of sodium laureth sulfate (a surfacant cleaning agent used in expensive salon shampoos), hundreds of Web sites and chat rooms dedicated to informing you about hair loss remedies, and even scores of sites dedicated to the classic rock musical Hair.

Admittedly, the dearth of information can be quite confusing, and perhaps more than a bit overwhelming. Added to that, many of those sites are really intended as promotions for expensive tonics, drugs, and products that promise startling results, but in most cases deliver disappointment, dangerous and unwelcome side effects, as well as a loud, annoying sucking sound as your money gets pulled down the drain.

This book is offered to you as an informative resource to answer your questions about hair care. In the pages that follow, you will find a lot of information gleaned from nearly thirty years of hands-on research in the field of tricology, the study of hair. Included are many suggestions and methods for improving the health of your "crown of glory," while addressing the specific requirements of your particular hair type. Some of this may seem to be common sense, but much of it will be quite surprising.

Most people have a visceral response to their own hair loss or damage that incorporates the belief that the problem must be localized somewhere between the follicle and the ends of their hair. Or, they say, "That's just the way it is, so I guess I'll have to suck it up and live with it." Those conclusions, while completely understandable, are frankly an erroneous outcome of deductive reasoning, or resigned frustration and tolerance. In the pages that follow, you will discover that the condition of your hair and scalp is a direct manifestation of what is going on throughout your body. This book will not only offer healthy, viable, prudent solutions to your own particular condition by exploring alternatives to caring for your hair and scalp, but will also closely examine how what you put into your body (vitamins, minerals, foods, caffeine, cigarettes, herbs, etc.) can have a powerful impact on the health of your scalp. Simply put, you will be learning a new way of caring for your hair by including what happens throughout your body, from the tips of your toes to the ends of your hair shafts.

But, that is only the beginning. How you live your life does have an immense impact on your hair, as well. By inquiring into the role of exercise, diet, meditation, hypnosis, and other mind-body techniques in boosting your optimal well-being, we'll uncover many habits and patterns in the modern lifestyle that can have a devastating and detrimental effect on your scalp's vitality. The fixed, often unconscious habits of your daily routine are a significant contributing factor. You will discover that there are many simple, minor modifications to your habits and routines that will bear potent, healing results.

We'll also take a look at the predominant causes of hair loss, debunk some of the ubiquitous myths of Male Pattern Balding (MPB), and suggest several effective and alternative methods for halting the progress of hair loss without the risk of surgery, or uncertain prescription drugs and chemicals. You will also find a remarkably effective, comprehensive program— easily adaptable to your specific hair type and needs—that will stimulate the scalp to restore any remaining peach fuzz to its former full and healthy condition. If you're someone who is not suffering from this painful condition, you may be tempted to skip over those sections. Don't. The information, principles, and guidance will almost certainly be of value to you, and will expand your awareness of how hair works and how the body performs in generating a healthy scalp.

The advice offered in these pages is simple, practical, inexpensive, and safe, having been tested over and over again with thousands of people. Also included are many recipes for hair and skin cleansers, scalp stimulators, astringents, and formulas for exfoliating dead tissue and unwanted particles that clog the follicles, effectively stunting the vitality of your hair—all of which you can prepare right in your own kitchen with ingredients you probably already have in your cupboards and refrigerator. If you don't know how to cook, don't worry. The recipes are about as complicated as boiling water and stirring with a spoon. (A word to the wise: Before including any of the formulas and recipes presented in these pages as part of your regular daily routine, it is suggested that you test them with small amounts to make certain there is no allergic reaction.)

When you were born, you had the capacity to live your entire life with a full head of healthy, attractive hair. This book is intended to guide you so that you can fulfill on that capacity which has not until now been realized. While much of the material may appear to be aimed specifically at people who are losing hair, or going bald, it is really intended for everyone. The principles explored in the care of your scalp—hair care, skin care, diet, nutrition, exercise, and mind-body techniques—are applicable to anyone interested in having a healthy, full head of hair, anyone interested in restoring their crown of glory.

There is one caveat to those who are experiencing a condition of balding: If the hair follicles have completely stopped producing hair, this is not something that can be reversed. No one, not even the purveyors of Rogaine or Minoxidil, can change this. However, the program described in these pages will stop the progression of baldness. And, wherever you can still feel the peach fuzz, there is hope. By rigorously following this program—which takes a decidedly unconventional, yet pragmatic approach toward altering your relationship to your body by taking into account the interdependence of how you care for your hair, what you put into your body, and the consequences of your current lifestyle—your peach fuzz can be returned to its full, healthy, natural state.

First things first, though. Let's take a look at hair, discover what it is, and examine some of the common reasons for hair loss and other associated problems.

How Hair Works
Getting to the Root of the Hair

As Francis Bacon once said, "Knowledge is power." Most people really know very little about how their bodies work, usually deferring this knowledge to a need-to-know basis when a medical crisis arises. Certainly, this holds true when it comes to hair. If you're like the average Joe or Jane, you're probably quite content to wash it, comb it, and style it without ever giving a thought to what "it" actually is, or how it functions—until the day a friend gives you a snapshot they took of you at a recent party, or you look in the mirror and realize there's more hair in the washroom basin than on your scalp.

While you may be tempted to skip ahead to find out how to stop that receding hairline or repair those split ends, don't do it. This chapter will provide you with some critical and fundamental information about the structure of hair, and will be the basis for much of what is contained in the pages that follow. A little knowledge in the discipline of tricology, the study of hair and root, will empower you to make informed and sensible decisions about your specific condition, allowing you to get the most out of the advice offered in these pages.

Upon close examination of the human body, you'll notice that virtually every part is adorned with hair. The only areas that are not covered are the lips, parts of the genitalia, soles of the feet, nipples, and palms of the hands. In fact, the human body contains more hair follicles per square inch on the surface of the skin than do most other primates in the animal kingdom. You might think that monkeys and apes are hairier, but this is a fallacy. Monkeys and apes simply have hair that is coarser and longer, but they don't have more hair.

We have two general types of hair: a vellum hair that is extremely fine, and in many parts of the skin is virtually invisible to the naked eye. The second, more noticeable, is classified as terminal, which can be found on the head, eyelids, face, pubic area, armpits, and on the chests of males.

The terminal fibers on the scalp are distinguishable by a set of different sub-types. The hairline begins from the base of the neck with a very fine fringe of terminal hairs that surround the circumference of the head, giving a subtle progression from the vellum fibers of the supposedly "bare" skin to the thicker terminal hairs adorning the crown.

Each hair shaft stems from a tiny gland under the epidermis called the sebaceous gland. The sebaceous gland produces a yellow, fatty secretion called sebum, which acts as a lubricant for the hair. (Sebum is the substance that causes oily skin and, thus, is a contributing factor in the formation of acne.) The hair shaft and sebaceous gland are surrounded by tiny erector pili muscles, which connect the base of the hair shaft to the underside of the skin. These erector pili contract, effectively squeezing the sebaceous gland and causing the gland to lubricate the hair with sebum. (You probably have felt the erector pili muscles in your arms contract when someone has told you a good ghost story, or you've gotten goose pimples from a winter chill.)

The skin from which our hair arises is comprised of three distinct layers, the epidermis, the dermis, and a layer of subcutaneous fat and connective tissue.

The epidermis is composed of dead skin cells, and is generally about one millimeter in depth. The dead cells are in a constant state of sloughing, being replaced by newer dead cells when they fall off.

The second layer, the dermis, is roughly two to three millimeters thick on your scalp. This tough layer of connective tissue is where the sebaceous glands are located.

Below the dermis is more connective tissue, accompanied by a layer of subcutaneous fat. The blood vessels that nourish the skin are nestled here amongst millions of sensory nerve branches. On the scalp, this is the layer in which you will find the bulbous terminal hair follicles numbering on average from 100,000 to 150,000. Each hair follicle measures three to four millimeters in length, and, just like the skin, has three layers: The Trichelemma (the pore from which the hair emanates), an inner root sheath, and the cuticle. This cuticle is the apparatus by which the hair shaft is held to the scalp.

At the base of the follicle is a tiny organ called the papilla, which extends up through the center of the follicle to the bottom of the hair. The papilla is what actually produces hair cells. A healthy papilla will become engorged with blood, from which it synthesizes proteins and formulates keratin, a protein comprised of a combination of carbon, hydrogen, nitrogen, sulfur, and oxygen. This protein forms 97% of the hair cells, which are forced up through the follicle, pushing up the older cells until they emerge from the scalp as your hair growth. The remaining 3% of the shaft is made up of amino acid, minerals, and a few other trace elements.

The hair shaft itself is also comprised of three layers of cells.

The outermost layer, called the cuticle, is composed of complex, interlocking scale-like cells. These cells can be chemically stimulated to be raised, allowing for the absorption of moisture. This is in fact what happens when you use a conditioner, or have your hair colored, bleached, straightened, or curled. When hair is referred to as "damaged," the cuticle layer is where most of this "damage" has occurred.

The cells of the cortex, the second layer of the hair shaft, are elongated, providing strength and flexibility. The cortex also contains the pigmentation, which gives the hair its natural color.

The round cells of the third layer, the medulla, are the marrow of the hair shaft, and are frequently not found in hair that is very fine.

Hair grows in stages. At any given moment, about 90% of the terminal hairs on your scalp are presently growing at a rate of about one-half inch per month. These hairs are in the anagen stage, a period which commonly lasts from two to seven years. The remaining 10% are in a dormant state called telogen, which normally lasts for about three months. During this resting phase, the papilla stops producing keratin, and the hair shaft detaches from the gland, eventually falling from the scalp. A new hair will take its place when the papilla returns to the anagen stage.

When the growth cycles from anagen to telogen to anagen again are functioning properly, most people should lose an average of eighty to one hundred hairs per day. Anything more than that indicates that something is awry.

Which leads us to the end of our introductory course in tricology. Now that you have a basic understanding of the physiology of hair and how it works, let's turn to the more advanced topics of the causes of hair loss and other common issues.

The Causes of Hair Loss and Other Problems

How to Stop Hair Loss

With a rudimentary understanding of the physiology of hair behind us, we can now begin to turn our attention to the subject that is the concern of so many men and women, and is probably one of the primary reasons you're holding this book right now: the subject of hair loss.

Before we can begin to address the solutions to this all too common affliction, an understanding of the fundamental types of hair loss, and their causes, will be crucial to the implementation of any successful hair restoration program.

To reiterate, losing hair is normal. Most people lose between eighty to one hundred terminal hairs per day from their scalp. This is even true of the majority of people who are experiencing hair loss or thinning, known as alopecia ("al-oh-pee-sha"). When the follicles of people suffering from alopecia shift into the dormant telogen period, the hair falls out at the same rate as healthy people. The difference is that the follicle closes up and shuts down rather than reawakening to the active anagen stage. There are some types of alopecia that result in elevated rates of shedding, often losing whole clumps of hair at a time, but this condition is rare and we'll discuss this in further detail a bit later.

There are several classifications of alopecia, with the most prevalent being androgenetic alopecia, the culprit in over 95% of hair loss cases. Both men and women experience androgenetic alopecia. For men it is often pronounced and dishearteningly visible for all the world to see, and is commonly referred to as Male Pattern Baldness (MPB). In women, it is usually fairly diffuse, occurring over broader regions of the scalp, resulting in an overall thinning of the hair rather than the development of any discernible pattern of baldness.

Androgenetic alopecia is widely recognized as a genetic trait passed down from either parent. This is why it is known as "pattern" baldness, since the same patterns tend to show up throughout the family tree. The genetic code for hair loss sends hormone messages to the cells in the follicles associated with the family pattern. The hormone messages essentially tell the papilla in these follicles to grow thinner and lesser hair, eventually shutting them down until they grow no hair at all.

Those hormones that direct the hair follicles are part of an extensive assortment of hormones called androgens. Testosterone and estrogen, present in both men and women, are without a doubt the best-known androgens, and play essential roles in the genetic code's mandate for pattern hair loss. Hormone levels deviate from person to person, and fluctuate at different stages their life.

As the blood carries testosterone to the hair follicle, it interacts with an enzyme called 5-alpha reductase, converting the hormone into dihydrotestosterone (DHT). DHT restricts the vasodilatation (blood flow) to the papilla at the base of the follicle. In short, it is the culprit androgen hormone that provokes hair loss, hence androgenetic alopecia.

Estrogen is a known androgen that obstructs the effects of DHT. Since women have higher levels of estrogen than men do, most women are safeguarded from androgenetic alopecia—that is until they reach menopause, when the levels of estrogen take a sudden, sharp drop in the bloodstream. With the DHT newly unimpeded, the onset of hair thinning in menopausal women can sometimes be quite dramatic in its rapidity.

Before losing heart, there is one other important factor to keep in mind: The genetic code merely determines a *tendency* toward DHT's vasodilatation of the papilla. If unchecked, hair loss will certainly result. However, there are many methods for interrupting this process, and we'll explore some of them in the next chapter.

Another form of hair loss is traction alopecia, which occurs when the hair shafts are subjected to the constant pulling of tightly braided hairstyles, plucking, tweezing, and waxing. This traumatizes the follicles, and leads to the hairs falling out before the completion of their growth cycle. Usually, traction alopecia is temporary, taking three to four months for the follicles to recover. Nonetheless, repeatedly subjecting the same follicles to this constant pulling will eventually lead to permanent hair loss.

About 1% of the population suffers from a condition called alopecia areata, an autoimmune condition in which the white blood cells interpret the hair follicles as an invading tissue that must be expelled from the body. Alopecia areata customarily causes people to lose hair on the scalp in smooth, circular clumps typically about one inch in diameter. In severe cases this can expand to the loss of all scalp hair (alopecia totalis), and sometimes expands to the loss of all hair on the body (alopecia universalis). Typically, this incurable autoimmune complication is temporary, though its duration is entirely unpredictable.

Telogen effluvium is a form of hair loss resulting from sudden severe stress. This can be a rather traumatic occurrence because the shedding of hair is always delayed, in most cases three to four months and sometimes as much as six months *after* the originating stressful event (i.e., a job termination, divorce, death of a loved one). Telogen effluvium strikes randomly across the scalp, and is most often noticeable only to the person suffering from the infliction. It is temporary, since there has been no damage to the follicle. Most of the hairs will return once the normal anagen and telogen growth cycles resume.

Childbirth can provoke telogen effluvium, but not because it is a stressful event (which it certainly can be for many women). It's really triggered by sudden changes in hormones after giving birth. During pregnancy, estrogen levels surge sufficiently to inhibit the dormant telogen period in a considerable percentage of the scalp. This is why pregnant women notice that their hair seems fuller. It is because there are more active follicles growing hair. Immediately following childbirth, those follicles that usually would have been dormant suddenly get the message that its time for a rest. Within a few months some new mothers will begin to shed hair, sometimes in distressing quantities.

Pregnancy terminations, abortions and miscarriages, can also result in telogen effluvium if enough of the woman's hair follicles have missed their telogen period.

Discontinuing the use of certain contraceptive pills sometimes has the side effect of triggering telogen effluvium, since many of these drugs operate by adding hormones to the woman's blood stream. Essentially, they work by fooling the reproductive system into thinking the woman is already pregnant, thus raising the estrogen levels and further inhibiting the telogen period. Once the dosage of the drug is stopped, the normal growth cycles kick in and there is the resultant telogen effluvium.

Anagen effluvium is the abrupt loss of hair from the chemicals and radiation treatments prescribed for cancer patients. Quite the opposite of telogen effluvium where the hair loss begins after three or four months, the hair loss of anagen effluvium commences within one to three weeks after a treatment. These patients can expect that either some, or all, of their hair will fall out. Chemotherapy and radiation therapy work by killing the rapidly dividing cells characteristic of cancer. Unfortunately, the treatment also kills other rapidly dividing cells such as the ones being produced by the papilla in the hair follicles. In most cases, this condition is temporary, and within six months to a year the hair will begin to regrow.

Nutritional deficiencies play a large factor in hair loss and health. The human body is essentially comprised of three basic types of tissues: carbohydrates, fats, and proteins. Remembering that the hair shaft is made up of 97% protein, it is useful to realize that the processes for synthesizing proteins requires a great deal more energy than that of carbohydrates and fats. When a person is malnourished or ill, the hair stops growing, and the hair shafts will begin to look less and less healthy. The condition of the hair is a direct manifestation of a person's health.

Hair shaft breakage, damage to the hair itself, can also result in hair loss. Several things can cause breakage. One of the worst offenses is the use of hair styling chemicals, particularly the inexpensive isopropyl alcohol-based gels, sprays and mousses you can find at just about any supermarket, or drug and thrift store. Hair dyes, bleaches, relaxers (straighteners most frequently used by African-Americans), and permanent wave solutions can wreak a lot of damage, especially if you use them with any sort of regularity.

Blow dryers and curling irons can make the hair shaft highly prone to breakage. Excessive heat causes the shafts to become weak and brittle.

Improper grooming techniques cause damage, as well. Using a comb or brush when your hair is wet, and at its weakest, should never be done. In fact, never use a brush on wet hair. Use a wide-toothed comb, or your fingers! (More about brushes will come later.)

Men who part their hair are particularly susceptible to hair loss. Parting the hair, which is usually done with a comb while the hair is wet, causes a weakening of the follicles and hair shafts in the crown where the hair is combed. Again, use of a wide-toothed comb, or, better yet, your fingers, is strongly urged.

Excessive shampooing with inexpensive store-bought products can dry out your hair, making it brittle and near to the point of breakage. The same can be said for vigorous shampooing, improper scalp massage, or towel-drying techniques.

Chlorine and sunlight weaken the hair shafts, too. When swimming, you should cover your scalp with a swimming cap to avoid exposure. (If you don't like the idea of a swimming cap, then wash your hair immediately upon leaving the pool, or ocean.) Moreover, when going out into the bright sunlight, wearing a hat will block the damaging rays of the sun.

Perhaps the most important factor in hair loss is how almost every single one of the conditions described above affect the sebaceous gland and it secretion of the lubricating sebum. What happens 99% of the time (particularly in MPB), whether the papilla's production of keratin is disrupted by the genetic balding messages carried in DHT, or the hair shaft has suffered breakage from too much bleaching, sebum begins to build up in the follicle. The follicle then becomes blocked, inducing further damage to the tiny structure and effectively cutting off any chances for the hair to survive. This, in fact, is the literal root cause of hair loss.

Now, let's turn to perhaps the most controversial section of this book: the various methods prevalently employed to restore hair by treating the conditions and symptoms described in this chapter.

4

Drugs, Transplants and Surgery

Illusions of the Hair Loss Industry, The Business of Hair Loss

---

Imhotep, a royal priest who lived 4,000 years ago in the Old Kingdom of the Nile Valley, is regarded as the architect who originated the iconic design of the pyramids of Ancient Egypt. He is also commonly acknowledged as the father of medicine, with numerous unearthed medical papyrus texts being attributed to him. The Edwin Smith Surgical Papyrus, which is among the oldest writings ever discovered, has been dated at around 1700 BC, and is particularly noteworthy for encapsulating Imhotep's remarkable clinical precision.

Sadly, his keen sense of observation, empiricism, and no-nonsense results has not always been the keystone for the discipline of medicine. This has been particularly so for the practice of hair restoration. Indeed, even in Imhotep's own kingdom one can find such ludicrous prescriptions as a compound constituted from the dung of a hippopotamus with liberal dollops of crocodile fat in equal parts which was then applied directly to the scalp. Almost a thousand years later, Hippocrates, who fostered the enduring medical ethic known as The Hippocratic Oath, refined his Egyptian predecessor's prescription with a recipe calling for cumin, horseradish, nettles, and fresh pigeon droppings.

Things have improved only slightly over the ages, with many senseless (and even downright dangerous) methods and tonics being passed off as remedies for hair loss. Today, the search for a cure has ballooned to an industry with estimated annual earnings in excess of $7 billion dollars. To make matters worse, much of the industry is cloaked in the credible mantle of scientific research, funded by large drug manufacturers with slick and comforting ad campaigns churned out by executive committees in glass towers lining the New York skyline along Madison Avenue. Frankly, they're not too far removed from the snake-oil salesmen slithering through the frontiers of the Old West.

What these massive pharmaceutical and surgical corporations are not willing to state up front in their glossy print ads and cozy primetime 30 second spots is this: They don't have a cure. They don't even understand for certain why DHT shuts down keratin production in the papilla. In effect, all they are selling is a treatment for the *symptoms* by fending off the inevitable progression of further hair loss. And, if you ever stop using their drugs, or don't check in for additional surgery, your condition will regress to the way it was before you started, often rapidly degenerating to a worsened predicament.

To put it bluntly, the only guarantee they can offer with impunity is that your bank account will be seeing a lot more red ink.

Currently the Food and Drug Administration (FDA) has approved only two drugs for wide use in the United States: Minoxidil, commonly sold under the registered trademark name Rogaine, and finasteride, a daily pill marketed as Propecia.

Minoxidil was originally introduced as a treatment for high blood pressure. This drug is prescribed for hypertensive patients only as an option of last resort since it is known to have some very severe side effects: chiefly chronic fluid retention, which eventually results in congestive heart failure.

Another less threatening side effect became apparent shortly after it was introduced: patients began growing hair in some pretty peculiar places, such as the backs of their hands and foreheads. After an intuitive leap of logic, and more testing in the Upjohn science labs, it turned out that minoxidil regrew hair when applied as a topical crème on the partially balding scalps of men with none of the life-threatening side effects of the oral version.

It does not work on areas of the scalp that are completely bald, where the follicles have died. Neither does it appear to have any regrowth effects on the front part of the scalp. Furthermore, minoxidil's restorative properties appear to be temporary at best. Eventually, the DHT levels in the bloodstream build up a resistance and overpower any benefits the drug bestows. With time, the patient will resume going bald.

Other problems include the fact that results are frequently not visible for at least six to twelve months—that's only if it's applied twice a day *without fail*. Additionally, minoxidil has difficulties being absorbed into the follicles of the scalp, so it is frequently manufactured with Retin-A, a topical retinoic acid which acts as a conductive. Retin-A increases the absorption levels of minoxidil, but it too has side effects. It commonly causes skin irritation, rashes, infection, and scarring, all of which ironically enough lead to permanent hair loss.

Finasteride, manufactured by Merck under the trademark Propecia, is only somewhat of an improvement over minoxidil. Originally, it was designed to treat benign prostate hyperplasia, and, like minoxidil, it too had the unexpected side effect of inducing hair growth. Merck's science team discovered that cutting the prostate medication to a one-fifth dosage was sufficient for the treatment of hair loss. Since it is a pill taken once a day, as opposed to a crème applied twice a day, it's easier to manage the dosages.

Following the adage that less is more, however, Propecia costs two to four times the price of Rogaine.

That's not the only side effect, either.

Impotence, diminished libido, and a decreased volume of ejaculate are experienced in some men, as well as gynecomastia, an enlargement of the breasts. (Although women may think this might be a desirable side effect worth obtaining a prescription for, it should be noted that this condition occurs only in men.) Propecia also lowers prostate specific antigens (PSA) in the bloodstream, making it extremely difficult for the detection of prostate cancer. Women of child-bearing years should not touch any crushed tablets of the drug with their bare fingers or skin, as it is also known to cause severe birth defects.

The good news is that most of the side effects will disappear within a few weeks after discontinuing the use of Propecia. The bad news is that you'll lose all the hair you regrew within two to six months. So, once you've started using Propecia, *you can never stop.*

Moreover, the FDA, which was commissioned with the responsibility of determining the safety and *effectiveness of* medications distributed in the United States, uncharacteristically approved Propecia *without the benefit of any long-term studies on its effectiveness.* (In fact, it certainly appears the potential revenue that would eventually be earned by Merck persuasively eclipsed any reasonable scientific methodology the FDA applied in its decision-making process.) No one knows if the DHT's in the bloodstream will build up a resistance, like minoxidil, and overpower the drug. It's simply too early to tell.

Currently, there are several other potential drugs in various testing stages with the FDA, some of which are intended for prescription use by women. Without exception, though, these newer drugs do have side effects ranging from mild and reversible reduction of testosterone levels in men, and progesterone in women, to toxic, irreversible damage to the liver.

Surgical treatments for hair loss have enjoyed a surge in popularity, and the consequent leap in profits, due to vast improvements in technology over the last ten years. Though hair restoration specialists can now be found in virtually every medical clinic around the corner, the results have not improved by much.

Slick advertising is used to sell the idea that surgery is now the answer to hair restoration. This is a blatant canard to state it mildly. No new hair is added to the scalp. It's simply moved from the areas that aren't (apparently) programmed for androgenetic alopecia, giving the *illusion* of more hair. Be it a micro-graft, full-sized hair plug, scalp lift or reduction, *it does not stop hair loss. Period.*

For surgery to produce convincing results, it typically requires several procedures, each of which must be administered three to four months apart. Each procedure can cost anywhere from a couple of thousand dollars to as much as $20 thousand or more. Most insurance companies categorize hair restoration as an elective procedure and therefore do not pay out any benefits; so most patients must finance the surgery with credit cards or a second mortgage. (Oddly enough, one of the selling points of surgery is that it supposedly costs less than drug treatments spread out over a lifetime.)

The use of laser technology has been heavily promoted in recent years with assurances of less time in the operating room, and reduced cosmetic complications such as scarring, bumps, or depressions that commonly result from the old-style metal instruments. But, lasers are an expensive investment, which has assuredly tempted many a surgeon to aggrandize their benefits in an attempt to pay them off. The cost of the hardware is passed on to the patient.

The surgeon rarely passes on complete information to the patient such as the vital drawbacks of laser surgery that might cause a patient to seek assistance elsewhere: The laser burns a tiny hole in the scalp, where the redistributed hair follicle is to be placed. The hole is very precise, which is the major selling point of laser surgery. This hole is supposed to heal faster and cleaner than the holes made from old-style metal instruments. Nevertheless, because the burst of light is required to be quite intense, it often burns additional cells immediately surrounding the hole. This slows the natural fibrin bonding process, which is the first stage of healing when a new follicle is inserted. The follicle takes longer to reconnect to the blood supply, increasing the risk of a lower yield of hair growth.

Essentially, the patient has paid for a really expensive light show.

Artificial hair transplants are available in Japan and some European countries. Although recent developments have produced extremely realistic synthetic hairs that produce marvelous and immediate cosmetic results, there are some serious drawbacks. The FDA has banned this procedure since 1984 because, in every single case, the body's immune system eventually rejects the synthetic hairs as a foreign substance. Often, chronic inflammation and bacterial infections in the scalp accompany the immune response, leading to infection of living hair follicles and increased hair loss.

Doctors in Japan, Mexico, and a few European countries also offer a surgical procedure for attaching a hairpiece that can be removed for ease of cleaning. The hairpiece is attached most commonly with osseo-integrated pins. These pins are made of titanium and are permanently imbedded into the skull. Bone tissue grows around the pins over time, fastening them securely. The hairpiece, which looks very realistic, is fitted with metal snaps that attach to the pins. The only problem with this procedure is that it is *extremely* dangerous. Any operation that entails cutting into the skull is considered risky. Leaving a foreign object in the skull, even surgical-grade titanium, which is exposed to the outside environment of the scalp, is playing with rather dicey odds stacked in favor of a lethal brain infection. The surgery required to remove the pins is even more dangerous than implanting them.

$7 billion a year is generated in the United States alone by the treatments described above. Not one of them actually addresses the source of the problem, attacking it from only one narrow viewpoint, or, as in the case of surgery, avoiding a genuine solution altogether. The human body is a complex machine, with all of its parts elegantly integrated into a wondrous whole.

When viewed from this wondrous whole, a solution does in fact present itself. A solution that is in perfect alignment with the natural processes of the human organism, and improves not just the health of the scalp, but also the well-being of the entire body. As we said in the previous chapter, the body is composed of carbohydrates, fats, and proteins, with hair being 97% protein. The condition of the hair is a direct reflection of the condition of the whole body. Simple intuitive logic argues that a program that addresses hair care from a holistic perspective will obtain results that permanently interrupt further hair loss, improves the condition of the hair, the overall health of the body, and quality of life.

This holistic perspective is one that pharmaceutical and surgical companies have ignored and derided in the interest of elevated profits. What follows in the remaining sections of this book is a program that will empower you toward a solution that will actually get to the root, so to speak, of the problem, and won't require a second mortgage on your house.

It will require an unerring level of rigor. The program, once it begins, must be followed *exactly* as prescribed. Any deviance from the program will disrupt the process, and you will have to start again. The program will also require a transformation in thought. There will be ideas and techniques that will challenge your thinking, sounding rather fantastic and unusual. Trust may be the key word here. The program has been tested and refined on thousands of clients over the past thirty years. Every one of them would tell you the same thing: "The program works."

It will also require a transformation in lifestyle. You will discover that there are certain practices that you currently have in your life which don't support your health, and more directly don't support the health of your hair. The program suggests simple ways to alter, or remove, these practices, while greatly improving your quality of life.

So, take a deep breath, and let's begin.

5

The Program

A Brief Overview of
Things to Come
A Prescription for
Healthy Hair

As we have seen in the previous chapter, merely attacking the symptoms of hair loss or damage really does nothing to resolve the condition. In fact, what is required is nothing short of a full-body transformation. A healthy functioning body is tantamount to generating a healthy head of hair. If that sounds like a lot of work, it really isn't. Affecting a full-fledged transformation does not necessarily require a huge effort. Sometimes the simplest steps can move the world, much like the great Greek mathematician Archimedes did with his famed fulcrum. For most people the hardest part will be the effort to maintain vigilance and rigor in sticking to the program.

Is it difficult? No.

The program that follows is actually very simple. All of the techniques and tips can be incorporated into your daily routine with a great deal of ease. Many suggestions are included to assist you in making the program an ordinary part of your day-to-day life.

As reinforcement for your commitment, it is strongly recommended that you invite your spouse, children, or life-partner to participate in the program with you. Change is always easiest when you have the full support of those closest to you. Since the program is designed to promote vitality and health throughout the whole body, they will assuredly reap benefits just as extraordinary as your own healthy head of hair. Included are many variations and much information specifically addressing the needs of each member of your family, whether they are suffering from a form of alopecia, split ends, or simply want to enhance the condition of their hair.

Remember that we are intending on stimulating the vitality of the entire body by filtering out the toxins, while increasing its capacity for absorption of vital proteins, minerals, and vitamins. This particularly includes cleansing, stimulating, and optimizing the bloodstream that is integrally tied to the follicles of the scalp, and there is a multitude of workable steps available toward that end. Those steps will be explained and clarified over the next several chapters.

THE FIRST STEP

Ready for the first step of the program? It's a big one, and it's probably the most difficult...

Now, go to your bathroom. Collect all of your hair care products, your shampoos, conditioners, gels, mousses, sprays, relaxers, dyes... Everything. Including the expensive products your stylist sold you during your last trip to the salon.

Next, throw them away.

Yes, that's right. *Throw them away*. (Or rather, rinse them out and recycle the containers.) Those over-the-counter items are another one of the causes of hair damage and loss.

Take a look at the ingredient label on your favorite bottle of shampoo before you toss it in the recycling bin. Whatever is shown first on the list is what there is the most of in the bottle, and what comes at the end of the list is what's least. The first ingredient will almost certainly be water ("eau," if the manufacturer's marketing department has settled on building the snob appeal by including a French translation). Second or third on the list will be a chemical surfactant, which is intended to help the cleaning agents lather more, or they can also be the primary cleaning agent. The two common surfactants used in shampoos are ammonium laurel sulfate, and sodium laureth (or laurel) sulfate. Ammonium laurel sulfate is used in most cheap or inexpensive shampoos from your drug store or grocery. Sodium laureth sulfate, which is gentler, is used in most salon products, and is the primary reason they are more expensive than your drug store shampoo. (If you bought a product from a salon with ammonium laurel sulfate, you can rest assured that you got ripped off.) The salon products also probably include one or two high-quality protein conditioners, which also accounts for their higher cost.

The remaining ingredients on the label are intended as preservatives, or for consumer appeal: A pleasant color to the shampoo, aroma, and whatever the latest buzzword is in the marketing world, i.e., aloe, honey, or the current herbal scent. (Yes, honey and herbs are wonderful ingredients to use on your hair, but not in the minimal quantities used in a shampoo purchased from a store or salon. Aloe can also be good, too, but only if it is stabilized aloe. Otherwise it's just a clever way of selling more water.)

Many of these over-the-counter shampoos and conditioners leave a heavy silicon-like deposit under the cuticle of the hair shaft. Eventually, it leaves enough deposits to cause breakage, and is the reason most people feel they have to change shampoos every few months.

For those of you who use a dandruff shampoo, throw that away too (unless you have a prescription from your doctor): You have been duped by the shampoo industry into believing you have dandruff. Most likely you don't. Almost nobody actually has dandruff. The industry marketing departments have done a stellar job of selling the idea that a flaking scalp is caused by dandruff. It's not! The only cause of flaking is having a dry scalp. Dandruff is a rare condition of oily, yellow or gray powder clumping together to form tiny balls—never flakes. Once you start on the program, your flaking scalp will be healed very quickly, so throw that bottle away immediately.

Now that you've taken the first step of the program by discarding everything in your bathroom, you will need something to replace all of those products: The program includes scores of recipes for shampoos, rinses, conditioners, and styling gels that are 100% natural, can be made right in your kitchen, and can be readily adjusted for the specific needs of each member of your family. If you don't know how to cook, don't worry. Pretty much all you need to know how to do is boil water, and do a little stirring and mixing. That's it.

You will also need to take a trip to the supermarket or health food store. Buying all of the ingredients at the start of the program may seem like a considerable expense initially, but most of the recipes are extremely concentrated. In a very short time, you will see that you're saving a substantial amount over the cost of the hair care products and restoratives you were buying before.

A FEW WORDS ABOUT PLANTS & HERBS

Open your dictionary and you'll probably find that its definition of the word "plant" probably refers to an organism in the vegetable kingdom with cell walls made of cellulose, and which transmutes inorganic substances (i.e., carbon dioxide) in order to grow. Whatever the definition says, it will hardly do justice to the innumerable variety of species covering the globe, nor even the organisms from the vegetable kingdom we'll be utilizing during this program. Several of the upcoming chapters refer to various plants and herbs that are widely known for their properties of stimulating hair growth, restoring vitality, and enhancing the body's performance. It will greatly support your understanding of those plants and herbs by taking a moment to go over their basic physiology and some fundamental ways in which to prepare them for use.

A plant is essentially made up of five parts: roots, stems, leaves, flowers, and fruit. Roots can be found underground, and have two main duties: 1) they anchor the plant into the ground, and 2) they absorb water and nutrients from the soil.

Stems are a bit more complicated. Herbaceous perennials have stems that dwell underground, with roots that extend deeper into the soil from the bottom side of the stem. These kinds of stems are known as rootstocks. Stolon stems grow on the surface and send their roots down into the ground, much like a rootstock. Corm stems are short sticks, or bulbs, that live underground, storing food and producing an aerial stem, the type that most people probably think of as a stem (gladiola and tulip bulbs are good examples of corm stems). Aerial stems bear leaves, which supply the plant with food.

Green leaves, through the function of photosynthesis, process the energy of sunlight to combine simple substances absorbed from the soil and air and converting them into complex food matter. During photosynthesis, plants use up carbon dioxide and produce oxygen. Chlorophyll, a critical agent in this process, is the pigment that gives a green leaf its color. There are other pigments, but those colors are masked until the leaf dies and the chlorophyll breaks down.

The botanical function of flowers is reproduction. Born on a receptacle on the stem, the typical flower is made up of several parts: the calyx, a set of leaves that protect the flower before it opens; the corolla, a set of white or colorful leaves commonly called petals; the stamen, with is the male organ that provides fertilization in the form of pollen; and the very center of the flower, which is the pistil, the female organ that captures the pollen produced by the stamen.

Fruit has a much more extensive definition in botany than it does in the popular vernacular, but in essence it is the ripened ovary of a flower or flower cluster. Botanically speaking, nuts, beans, corn grains, tomatoes and dandelion seeds are just as much a fruit as figs, oranges, cherries, and lemons. The primary function of fruit is to disperse seeds through nature's boundless ingenuity in preserving and expanding life: wind, birds, humans, falling and rolling across the ground, etc.

It has been said that nature provides a remedy for every disease. Over the past twenty years, herbs have grown substantially in repute toward proving this aphorism to be true. To obtain herbs, you can take a trip to the wilds, grow them yourself, pull out the yellow pages and find an herb supplier in your neighborhood, or find a supplier on the Internet. The yellow pages are probably the easiest and quickest, especially since most health food stores, drug stores and super markets now carry extensive supplies of herbs. And, the Internet offers hundreds of good companies that sell almost anything you could ever want.

Herbs come in diverse forms, ranging from fresh, dried, or powdered, and can be prepared in many ways utilizing the various parts of these plants. The following types of preparations are the most commonly applied in herbal medicines. Not all of these methods will be employed in this program, but, as you explore the world of herbs and their myriad properties, it can be useful information:

> *Infusion:* An infusion is the process of making a tea-like liquid by steeping the plant parts (customarily the green parts or flowers) in boiling water, which extracts their active ingredients. The relatively short exposure to heat minimizes the loss of any vital healing properties. In many formulas, the hot water is poured over the herbs, but some call for the plants to be added to the boiling water; the pot should then be removed from the heat, or the heat is reduced depending upon the recipe. You should use either a glass, or enamel pot to steep the plants. Many metal pots will chemically interact with the herbs, negating their active ingredients. While allowing the herbs to steep for approximately ten minutes, the pot should be covered with a tight fitting lid to minimize evaporation.

Decoction: This process extracts primarily the mineral salts and bitter essences of herbs and plants, rather than the vitamins and healing properties. This is also the best method to be used when working with roots, bark, wood, and seeds. Most decoction formulas require that you boil about a half ounce of the plant per one cup of pure water in an enameled or glass pot. Boil them for about ten minutes, then cover and allow to steep for another ten minutes. Green plant parts can be added to boiling water and boiled for about four minutes before removing from the heat. Then, cover and let steep for another three minutes. Strain, and then store in a clean glass jar or squeeze bottle.

Cold extract: Preparation of a cold extract takes a lot longer than an infusion, but it is more effective at extracting and preserving the healing properties. Add about twice the measurement of herbs used in an infusion to cold water in an enameled or glass pot (again, metals can interfere with the herbs). Most formulas require that you let the concoction stand for about twelve hours. Then, strain and store in a clean glass jar or squeeze bottle.

Powder: Dried plant parts can be ground with a mortar and pestle to make a powder. This powder can be ingested with water, soups, juice, sprinkled on foods, or inserted into gelatin capsules and swallowed. You should do some research to determine the proper dosages for powder forms of any herb.

Tincture: A tincture is made by combining about one to four ounces of a powdered herb with about twelve ounces of grain alcohol. Pure water should be added to reduce the alcohol to a 50% solution (calculated by knowing what percentage of alcohol solution you started with). Pour into a glass jar with a tight lid, and let stand for one to two weeks depending upon the formula, giving the mixture a good shake once or twice a day. Then, strain and store in a clean glass jar or squeeze bottle. The alcohol content will preserve the tincture's healing properties for quite a long time.

Essence: Dissolving an ounce of an herb's essential oil in a pint of grain alcohol (vodka or rum) can make an essence, which is an excellent way of preserving the healing properties in the oils.

Ointment: Mixing one part herbs with four parts hot petroleum jelly can make an ointment. Or, you can infuse the herbs in boiling water, strain, then add the decoction to olive oil and simmer until the water has evaporated. Add beeswax for a firm consistency. Continue simmering until the mixture has melted, and stir until well blended. A small amount of gum benzoin, or a drop of tincture of benzoin per ounce, will preserve the ointment.

Poultice: A poultice can be used to apply herbal remedies directly to the skin with moist heat, soothing the body or drawing out impurities. Preparation begins by crushing the curative parts of the plants into a pulpy mass, then moistening with hot water, or combining with a hot mixture of flower or corn meal. (Use caution, making sure not to burn the skin.) The mixture is best applied by spreading the paste on a soft cloth and then wrapping it around the affected area. The cloth can continually be refreshed by periodically adding additional hot water. Upon removing the poultice, gently wash the skin with warm water to cleanse any remaining residues of the poultice.

Cold Compress: Many herbs can be used topically to heal conditions on the skin, or ailments just below the epidermis. A healing cold compress can be made by soaking a towel or cloth in a cool infusion or decoction. Wring out the excess liquid, and apply to an affected area on the skin for about 15 to 20 minutes. Reapply with a fresh compress and continue until the ailment is relieved.

Fomentation: A fomentation, or hot compress, is made in the same manner as a cold compress, except that the infusion or decoction is as hot as possible. Use caution, making sure not to burn the skin.

Light and oxygen are the two most formidable adversaries to preserving the effectiveness of herbs. They should be stored in clean, airtight jars made with dark glass, and kept in a cool, dry place. Dried herbs will inevitably lose their potency, so they should be replaced after a year.

WHAT TO EXPECT

The results of the program will be almost immediate. As new sets of follicles awaken from the dormant telogen state, many people who follow this program will see that they are growing in with voluminous, healthy hair shafts from the very first week. For others, it will take a little longer. In all cases, the full impact will not be seen for 52 weeks. While that may seem like a long time, it really isn't when you consider that the time to build up to your current condition of hair loss or damage probably took many years longer to develop. Restoring hair is never something that can happen over night. Nor is it something that can happen simply just because you want it, though that's a good place to start. It's going to take a little work, too.

But, there is so much more than that. As we pointed out in Chapter One, your hair is closely connected to your identity, and to how you feel about yourself. As you begin to see results, you will start to notice a transformation in your state of being, in your self-esteem. Your success cannot help but boost your sense of well-being, joy, dignity, and confidence. As you implement these suggested modifications to your lifestyle, you will begin to see extraordinary changes in how you feel about yourself. This program, time-tested with thousands of clients over thirty years, represents nothing less than the dawning of a whole new, unrecognizable you.

The Big Picture
Record Your Progress

Before we go any further, it's time to take a snapshot of where you're at right now. Literally.

When working with clients on the program, it is always best to begin by taking photographs so they can clearly see their progress over time. This is particularly important for keeping them grounded in reality. Over the course of a year, as you implement the life changes necessary for the transformation of your scalp, you will go through a lot of spaces. You'll probably start out the program with a heightened sense of gusto and commitment. Then, one day you'll wake up and wonder what the heck you're doing, and mutter at your reflection in the mirror, "What's the point? It's taking too long! I'm wasting my time!"

It's at moments like that where it's very useful to pull out your photos to see where you were when you started on Day One. There's nothing like a good dose of reality to jolt you out of the doldrums when you see that you've actually made a great deal of progress in a relatively short period of time. You will clearly see that all your hard work, dedication, commitment, and integrity have indeed been paying off. These photographs are a record of your success.

The camera doesn't lie. Having a clear, impartial measurement for your success like a photograph is an extremely useful tool for keeping on track and sticking with the program. Many clients over the years have attested to this, and have been thankful for the pictures.

These aren't portraits you'll be taking, so either a Polaroid or a digital camera will do. You'll also need a well-lit room, and a willing assistant (i.e., life-partner or spouse) to take the pictures.

1. Start by having your partner take a photo of your face from about the shoulder up. Be sure to leave room at the top of the frame for your entire scalp.

2 & 3. Next, take a shot of the right profile, then the left profile, making sure that the entire scalp is visible.

4. Take a shot of the back of your head from the shoulders up.

5. Finally, your partner needs to get a shot of the top of your head. You can either lean over by dropping your chin to your chest, or you can kneel on the floor.

In every shot, make certain your partner can clearly see the damage or areas of hair loss and thinning through the lens. If you can't see it when you print it out, or it develops, then it won't be much use as a measurement of your success.

If the camera did not indicate the date on the prints, then you need to date them yourself. Place the photographs in a small album, or glue them into a notebook. You'll be adding a new set of pictures every three months, so get out your calendar and schedule your photography sessions for the next twelve months. After the first 120 days, you will most likely already see a startling difference.

7

Shampoos
Healthy Formulas from Your Kitchen & Pantry

A few pages back, you were coached to throw away all your old hair care products. You need to replace those products with ones that will actually restore your damaged hair and promote hair growth. Let's start with the shampoos.

Before jumping into the actual formulas, a few words should be addressed to the subject of shampooing. Why shampoo? Shampooing removes the grime and dirt that builds up in your hair follicles as you move about through your day. For the papilla to function properly, that grime and dirt needs to be removed—daily. Additionally, your skin is constantly producing fresh skin cells, pushing the older, dead cells to the surface. Shampooing removes those dead cells from the scalp, allowing the skin to "breathe" properly. In short, you must shampoo each and every day. Period.

This is particularly important for people who are suffering from hair loss. Many people with this condition irrationally believe that shampooing aggravates the condition by accelerating the rate of alopecia, and choose to simply rinse their hair with plain water. This couldn't be further from the truth. Just watering the scalp rather builds up the level of sebum trapped in the follicles. Moreover, that sebum also traps the grime and dirt collected from every day life, eventually choking off the follicles and worsening the condition.

Set aside your fears. You must shampoo every day. Period.

When shampooing, remember to use your fingertips to massage the scalp and disperse the lather through the hair. Do not use the palms of the hands, as this could easily be too harsh and may cause breakage of the hair shafts, resulting in eventual hair loss. A gentle massage is an excellent way to invigorate the scalp, which increases blood flow to the papilla and stimulates hair growth. (More about massage later.) Rinse with cool or lukewarm water.

The formulas included below are very gentle, and don't work like the commercial shampoos you wisely disposed of. First of all, they may appear thinner than you're used to, and they don't leave your hair squeaky-clean. That "squeaky-clean" feeling was actually a result of those commercial shampoos stripping away every last ounce of protective oil from under the cuticles of the hair shafts, which does not promote the health of the hair shafts. These recipes will clean your hair of the excess oil and dirt, while conditioning your hair to feel soft.

In these recipes, we recommend starting with a bar of pure castile soap, which can be purchased at most major grocers or health food stores. All soaps are essentially made of either animal or vegetable fat combined with an alkali such as sodium hydroxide or potassium hydroxide. This combination engenders a chemical reaction called saponification: the process by which fat is turned into soap. Pure castile soap is usually made with excellent quality oils and fats, and a minimal amount of alkalis. Avoid castile soaps with additives, like almond oil, or scents. These can work against the positive effects of the herbs you'll be adding yourself, causing more damage.

This recipe is an Essential Formula and is merely a base from which to start. Following the recipe is a chart listing many readily available herbs that can be infused and added to the Essential Formula to adjust for all hair types and colors for each member of your family.

Essential Formula:
8 ounces pure water
Herb/s of your choice
2 cups pure water
1 bar pure castile soap

From the following chart of herbs, select the herbs for your particular hair type. Make an infusion by combining one teaspoon of each of the herbs of your choice in 8 ounces of boiling water. Turn off the stove, and let the herbs steep for about 6 hours. Strain and discard the remains of the herbs, then gently reheat water.

Bring 1 cup pure water to a rolling boil in a second pot. Shave the bar of pure castile soap with a knife or grater. Stir the soap shavings into the boiling water until fully melted.

Add two tablespoons of the melted castile soap to the warm herbal infusion, constantly stirring until well mixed. Dilute with additional pure water, as needed. Remove from heat and cool. Pour into a small jar, or squeeze bottle. Give it good shake before each use.

The remaining melted castile soap can be stored and saved for use as needed.

The chart below lists several useful herbs that can be infused and combined with the Essential Formula. The chart notes their common properties, and the general hair types for which they are most effective. You can select several combinations of herbs, and experiment to your own particular needs and taste. It is recommended that you make more than one shampoo so that you can alternate according to your hair type. For those with oily hair, you should rotate every other day with a shampoo specific for normal hair; otherwise, your hair will be stripped of all oils, becoming dry and brittle. For those with dry hair, you should alternate with a normal solution every other day as well. This will prevent your hair from becoming too oily, which will clog the follicles and lead to unwanted damage. People with normal hair should alternate between a normal solution, an oily solution, and a dry solution. This will help to keep your pH levels balanced.

Herbs and Their Properties	Normal	Dry Hair	Oily Hair
Burdock: Stimulates circulation of the scalp.	X	X	X
Chamomile: Anti-inflammatory properties; heals scalp irritations; is a natural hair tonic that also has a lightening effect, producing yellow highlights.	X	X	
Chaparral: Stimulates circulation of the scalp.	X	X	X
Comfrey: The leaves can heal irritated scalp conditions when used in an infusion.		X	
Elderflower: Anti-inflammatory properties; heals scalp irritations; gentle hair stimulant.	X	X	
Eucalyptus: Anti-inflammatory properties; heals scalp irritations; assists in regulating sebum production, and is a deep cleaning agent.			X
Garlic: Stimulates circulation of the scalp and promotes hair growth; heals scalp irritations, controls flaking, and heals eczema.	X	X	X
Horsetail: Stimulates circulation of the scalp; also a good source of silica, which promotes strength of hair shaft.	X	X	X
Indian hemp: Stimulates circulation of the scalp.	X	X	X
Lavender: Gentle hair stimulant; regulates pH levels; promotes body and shine of hair shaft; leaves a pleasant, soothing scent.	X		X
Lemon balm: Gentle cleansing herb that removes excess oil & sebum.			X
Lemon grass: Gentle cleansing herb that removes excess oil & sebum.			X
Lemon verbena: Cleanser and scalp stimulant.			X
Licorice: Contains a compound that prevents testosterone from being converted to DHT in men.	X	X	X
Marshmallow root: Has a potent conditioning and softening effect.		X	
Nettle (a.k.a., Stinging nettle): Stimulates circulation of the scalp, and is a cleanser.	X	X	X
Parsley: Promotes the health of the sebaceous glands; heals scalp irritations; conditions, and stimulates the hair.	X	X	X
Peppermint: Stimulates circulation of the scalp; acts as a gentle antiseptic.	X		X

Herbs and Their Properties	Normal	Dry Hair	Oily Hair
Red Clover: Gentle cleansing herb.		X	
Rosemary: Controls flaking and heals eczema; great for dark hair; also stimulates circulation of the scalp.	X	X	X
Sage: Helps reduce the level of sebum production in the sebaceous glands; stimulates circulation of the scalp.			X
Thyme: Cleansing & tonic properties; leaves a terrific scent.	X		X
Yarrow root: Helps reduce the level of sebum production in the sebaceous glands.			X

While not technically classified as herbs, aloe vera and jojoba can also be beneficial adjuncts to your shampoo formula. Stabilized aloe vera purchased in either a powder, gel, or concentrate works to strengthen the outer cuticle of the hair shafts, giving them a uniform, more reflective appearance—in short, promoting tangle-free, shiny hair. The antiseptic properties of aloe vera also work to heal the scalp and relieve it of eczema and flaking. Jojoba oil has long been acknowledged as a cure for many hair ailments, ranging from alopecia to eczema. Structurally, it is very similar to the sebum in your hair. This gives it the ability to attract and draw out unwanted sebum embedded in the follicles. Additionally, it tends to soothe the scalp, progressively decreasing excess sebaceous gland secretions, and heals irritations and flaking of the scalp.

You can try several combinations of the above herbs: lavender and rosemary with chamomile gives a nice herbal scent. Chamomile and marshmallow root are great for light hair, while sage, comfrey, and rosemary are excellent for darker hair. The chart below lists several useful herbs that can be infused and combined with the shampoo formulas in this chapter for particular hair colors:

Black hair:	Black henna, black malva, indigo, lavender; red henna or cloves can be added for reddish highlights
Blond or light hair:	Acacia flowers, black cherry bark, broom, calamus, chamomile, marigold, marshmallow root, orange flower, orris root, quassia chips, saffron, St. Johnswort, turmeric, yellow mullein flowers
Blue/White hair:	Bachelor button, blue malva, comfrey root, lavender (not to be used on dry hair), white chamomile flowers
Brown hair:	Aloe leaf, cassia bark, cloves, maidenhair, yarrow root
Brunette hair:	Cloves, comfrey leaf, jaborandi, lavender (not to be used on dry hair), marjoram, mint, quassia chips, raspberry, rosemary, sage, sassafras; also, herbs listed for brown or black hair
Gray/Dingy hair:	Hollyhock (turns dingy gray hair silver with bluish highlights)
Red hair:	Cloves, cochineal, marigold, red henna, red hibiscus, witch hazel bark

Willow leaves have been noted to strengthen hair, and stimulate an accelerated rate of growth. Here's another shampoo formula that also includes birch leaves, which are renowned for their unique ability to fortify the hair structure.

Willow & Birch Strengthening Formula:
6 cups pure water
1 cup willow leaves
1 cup birch leaves
6 tablespoons pure castile soap shavings

Bring the water to a boil, then add the willow and birch leaves. Cover; reduce the heat, then steep for no less than two hours. Remove from heat and let stand until cool. Strain and discard the leaves.

Gently reheat the infused water, and then add the pure castile soap shavings, constantly stirring until melted. Remove from heat and cool. Pour into a small jar, or squeeze bottle. Let the mixture stand at least 24 hours before first use. Always give it a vigorous shake before use.

To receive the maximum benefits of this strengthening formula, gently massage into your scalp and leave it in for ten minutes. Rinse thoroughly with cool or tepid water.

Comfrey root, nettles, peppermint, or quassia chips can be infused along with this formula to heal dry itchy scalps and eczema.

Raw egg, which is mostly protein, can give hair (which is 97% protein) a boost with extra body and shine. Beat 1 raw egg, and then combine with 1 tablespoon of either the Essential or Willow & Birch Strengthening Formulas. Shampoo as you would normally, but make sure you rinse your hair for at least one minute with cool or cold water. Warm water will poach the egg, leaving quite a mess in your hair. Since raw egg spoils quickly, it is recommended that you don't make this too far in advance. Be sure to refrigerate it, if you aren't going to use it immediately.

Pre-Shampoo for Dry or Damaged Hair
For chemically damaged hair, apply in the morning.

1 Tsp. Honey
2 Tsp. Olive Oil
1 Yellow of an Egg

Combine honey and olive oil until blended, adding beaten egg in slowly. With pastry brush, apply to hair in small strands. Wrap your hair in a hot towel (a shower cap will do), leave in for 15 minutes then shampoo in cool water, then warm.

Spice Rack Shampoo for Normal Hair
Add new flavor to your hair with this enhancing herbal blend.

1 Tbsp. Lavender
1 Tbsp. Sage
1 Tbsp. Rosemary
1 Tbsp. Parsley
4 Oz. Basic Shampoo
2 Drops Almond Oil
1 Qt. Distilled Water

Make in infusion of the lavender, sage, rosemary, parsley and water. Allow to sit overnight, then strain and filter. In a saucepan, add grated soap to infusion and heat until soap has dissolved. Allow to cool, then add almond oil and beat mixture. Pour shampoo into bottle and store. If soap hardens, gently heat bottle before using. This is an excellent cleanser, but do not expect a lather: this shampoo contains no detergent.

LemonAid Shampoo for Oily Scalp
3 Tbsp. Vodka
1 Tbsp. Lemon Juice
2 Oz. Castile Soap
1 Quart Distilled Water

Grate soap into 1 quart distilled boiling water, then lower heat until soap dissolves. In a blender, whip the mixture, then beat in the alcohol and lemon juice. Cool then shampoo. Store leftover in a labeled container.

Aromatic Dandruff Shampoo
8 Oz. Basic Shampoo
8 Drops Rose Geranium Oil
8 Drops Lemon Oil
8 Drops Rosemary Oil

Add oils into shampoo, shake well and apply.

Since the Egyptians invented it over 4,000 years ago, beer has been recognized to have the ability to give hair more bounce, body, shine, and can also be added to either the Essential or Willow & Birch Formulas. Heat 1 cup of your favorite beer (keep it to a light lager, like Rolling Rock, or Budweiser) in a saucepan. Bring it to a slow boil until the liquid is reduced to ¼ cup. Let it cool, and then stir in 1 cup of the shampoo of your choice. Store in a jar or squeeze bottle. Shampoo as you normally would.

Citrus fruits have the dual capacity of cleansing overly oily hair, and they act as a natural bleaching property. Their scent also has the added aroma-therapeutic effect of energizing and invigorating you. Don't use this formula more than once or twice a week. Over cleaning the follicles will trick the sebaceous glands into thinking they aren't doing their job, causing them to over-produce sebum and clog the follicles.

Energizing Citrus Formula
Peel of 1 grapefruit, lemon, and orange
6 cups pure water
¼ cup Essential Formula or Willow & Birch
　　Conditioning Shampoo
2 tablespoons grapefruit juice
2 tablespoons lemon juice
2 tablespoons orange juice

Slice the peels and puncture them with a knife or fork. Bring the water to a boil, then place the peels in the pan, stir and cover. Let it infuse for 2 hours. Strain the infusion to remove the peels. Mix in the shampoo and juices. Let it cool, and then store in a jar or squeeze bottle. Let stand for twenty-four hours before first use. Shake it vigorously before each use. It is recommended that you use this shampoo no more than once a week, unless followed by a moisturizing formula (See Chapter 8).

Stabilized aloe vera in greater quantities than the trace amounts in store-purchased shampoos can work as an excellent moisturizer, in addition to the properties discussed above.

Aloe Vera Moisturizing Formula
¼ cup Essential Formula or Willow & Birch
　　Conditioning Shampoo
¼ cup stabilized aloe vera gel
1 teaspoon glycerin
½ teaspoon avocado oil

Mix the ingredients together, then store in a jar or squeeze bottle. Give the bottle a good shake before each use. Shampoo as normal, though you may want to leave this on your scalp for about ten minutes before rinsing for maximal results.

Riquette lives by what she teaches.

Rinses & Conditioners
Healthy Formulas from
Your Kitchen & Pantry

CONDITIONERS

If nothing else, the hair care industry has trained us all in using a conditioner after shampooing. Shampoos are intended for cleansing by removing unwanted particles and oils. Conditioners are designed to restore the proteins and moisture to the hair cuticles, follicles, and scalp. However, the hair care industry has only given us part of the picture. Most conditioners available on the market are really just crème rinses intended for softening the hair, and contain synthetic silicone derivatives, such as Dimethicone, to detangle the hair for combing and brushing. Other ingredients commonly used in commercial conditioners include propylene glycol, isopropyl alcohol, formaldehyde, **FD & C Red Dye #4**, synthetic fragrance, mineral oil, petrolatum, and tallow, all of which build up in the hair shafts and lead to damage. There are plenty of natural products sold in many commercial conditioners, such as ginseng, aloe, green tea, plants, fruits, and flowers, but the quantities are insufficient to have any effect beyond enhancing the product's fragrance.

What is worse, the hair care industry has trained us all to believe a simple crème rinse is sufficient to maintain your hair. This is frankly not the case. Your hair care program should include *three* types of conditioners:

1) A crème rinse, not containing any of the products listed above, 2) A hair pack, applied only to your hair, and 3) A scalp pack that dries and absorbs excess oils and toxic particles, and is applied to just the scalp.

1.   **Crème Rinses**

Here is an Essential Conditioning Formula that can be used as a crème rinse three to four times a week, after shampooing.

> **Essential Conditioning Formula**
> 8 ounces pure water
> Herb/s of your choice
> 1 scoop powdered soy, or whey protein

Begin by making an herbal infusion from the chart of herbs below. Select the herbs for your particular hair type. Bring the water to a boil, and then add one teaspoon of each of the herbs of your choice. Turn off the stove, and let the herbs steep for about 6 hours. Strain and discard the remains of the herbs. Add protein powder, stirring until well-mixed.

Use only after shampooing by massaging onto the hair with your fingertips. If you have oily hair, apply to the ends of the hair only, avoiding the roots; administering it to your scalp will inadvertently increase the production of oil in the follicles. Let stand for three minutes, then rinse with cool or tepid water. Proceed with a rinse, described in the second half of this chapter.

Herbs and Their Properties	Normal	Dry Hair	Oily Hair
Burdock: Stimulates circulation of the scalp.	X	X	X
Chamomile: Anti-inflammatory properties; heals scalp irritations; is a natural hair tonic that also has a lightening effect, producing yellow highlights.	X	X	
Chaparral: Stimulates circulation of the scalp.	X	X	X
Comfrey: The leaves can heal irritated scalp conditions when used in an infusion.		X	
Elderflower: Anti-inflammatory properties; heals scalp irritations; gentle hair stimulant.	X	X	
Eucalyptus: Anti-inflammatory properties; heals scalp irritations; assists in regulating sebum production, and is a deep cleaning agent.			X
Garlic: Stimulates circulation of the scalp and promotes hair growth; heals scalp irritations, controls flaking, and heals eczema.	X	X	X
Horsetail: Stimulates circulation of the scalp; also a good source of silica, which promotes strength of hair shaft.	X	X	X
Indian hemp: Stimulates circulation of the scalp.	X	X	X
Lavender: Gentle hair stimulant; regulates pH levels; promotes body and shine of hair shaft; leaves a pleasant, soothing scent.	X		X
Lemon balm: Gentle cleansing herb that removes excess oil & sebum.			X
Lemon grass: Gentle cleansing herb that removes excess oil & sebum.			X
Lemon verbena: Cleanser and scalp stimulant.			X
Licorice: Contains a compound that prevents testosterone from being converted to DHT in men.	X	X	X
Marshmallow root: Has a potent conditioning and softening effect.		X	
Nettle (a.k.a., Stinging nettle): Stimulates circulation of the scalp, and is a cleanser.	X	X	X
Parsley: Promotes the health of the sebaceous glands; heals scalp irritations; conditions, and stimulates the hair.	X	X	X
Peppermint: Stimulates circulation of the scalp; acts as a gentle antiseptic.	X		X

Herbs and Their Properties	Normal	Dry Hair	Oily Hair
Red Clover: Gentle cleansing herb.		X	
Rosemary: Controls flaking and heals eczema; great for dark hair; also stimulates circulation of the scalp.	X	X	X
Sage: Helps reduce the level of sebum production in the sebaceous glands; stimulates circulation of the scalp.			X
Thyme: Cleansing & tonic properties; leaves a terrific scent.	X		X
Yarrow root: Helps reduce the level of sebum production in the sebaceous glands.			X

As with the shampoo formulas, the Essential Conditioning Formula is also a good opportunity to use herbs that enhance hair color through your herbal infusion:

Black hair:	Black henna, black malva, indigo, lavender; red henna or cloves can be added for reddish highlights
Blond or light hair:	Acacia flowers, black cherry bark, broom, calamus, chamomile, marigold, marshmallow root, orange flower, orris root, quassia chips, saffron, St. Johnswort, turmeric, yellow mullein flowers
Blue/White hair:	Bachelor button, blue malva, comfrey root, lavender (not to be used on dry hair), white chamomile flowers
Brown hair:	Aloe leaf, cassia bark, cloves, maidenhair, yarrow root
Brunette hair:	Cloves, comfrey leaf, jaborandi, lavender (not to be used on dry hair), marjoram, mint, quassia chips, raspberry, rosemary, sage, sassafras; also, herbs listed for brown or black hair
Gray/Dingy hair:	Hollyhock (turns dingy gray hair silver with bluish highlights)
Red hair:	Cloves, cochineal, marigold, red henna, red hibiscus, witch hazel bark

The following alternative crème rinse formula is excellent for dry and easily damaged hair, and should be used no more than once or twice a week. It is perishable and should be used immediately, yielding just enough for a single treatment.

Honey & Lemon Conditioning Formula
1 teaspoon almond oil
1 teaspoon avocado oil
1 teaspoon olive oil
1 egg yolk
1 tablespoon honey
1 tablespoon fresh lemon juice

Combine all of the ingredients and stir thoroughly. Use immediately.

Here's another one that is good for thin, dry and easily damaged hair suffering from split ends. The mixture of gelatin and egg makes an excellent protein and lecithin crème rinse formula for weekly use.

Gelatin & Egg Formula
1 tablespoon unflavored gelatin
¼ cup water
1 egg yolk
2 tablespoons fresh lemon juice

Gently warm the water, then stir in the gelatin until dissolved. Allow to cool, then add the egg yolk and lemon juice, stirring until well mixed.

After shampooing, massage the Gelatin & Egg Formula into your hair and let stand for two to three minutes. Rinse with cool water.

2. **Hair Packs**

There are several ingredients you can use straight from your kitchen that can be used as a protein hair pack to condition the hair. Mayonnaise, which is comprised mainly of egg, is perhaps the most common, easiest to find and provides an amazing measure of protein and restoration for the hair. Any one of the following ingredients may also be applied after shampooing:

Mayonnaise	Olive oil
Coconut oil	Plain yogurt
Mashed banana	Honey (for light or fair hair)
Mashed avocado	Molasses (for brown or
Raw egg	brunette hair)

For oily hair, add 2 teaspoons of fresh lemon juice to any of the above.

Gently massage for one to two minutes about ½ cup of any one of the above ingredients onto the hair shafts, taking care to avoid the scalp. Once thoroughly applied, you should cover your scalp with a plastic shower cap to lock in heat and stimulate the conditioning of the process. After at least fifteen minutes, rinse with cool water. (By the way, avocado skins are rich in Vitamin E, which is very good for the skin. After scooping out the avocado flesh, rub the skin on your face, elbows, or wherever you need it. Using the whole plant will give you more for your money's worth, and helps toward saving the environment.)

The Essential Conditioning Formula described in the crème rinses can be adjusted to make a conditioning pack by reducing the amount of water to 4 ounces. After mixing in your selection of protein powder, it should be applied to the hair shafts, taking care to avoid the scalp and roots. Wrap in tin foil and a shower cap (which captures the body's heat and activates the formula), and let stand for twenty to thirty minutes. Rinse with cool or tepid water. Once a month, you can go ahead and apply the pack to the scalp as well, using a fine toothbrush or pastry brush.

You can also try a once-a-week herbal oil treatment, which can be quite potent at restoring damaged hair with split ends.

Herbal Oil Treatment Formula
1 cup olive oil
1 cup peanut oil

4 ounces of herb/s of your choice (see charts above)
½ ounce rosemary or basil pure oil

Combine the olive and peanut oils with the herbs in a non-metal pot. Bring to a simmer, and continue heating until herbs are crisp. Strain the herbs, then pour 6 ounces of the infused oil into another bowl. Mix in the rosemary or basil oil.

Apply to the hair shafts, taking care to avoid the scalp and roots. Wrap your head in a warm towel, and then cover with a shower cap. Let stand for 1 hour. Rinse completely, then shampoo with a formula derived from Chapter 7. (This formula can also be used as a scalp pack, and is especially good for healing a dry, inflamed scalp. The condition can be cleared up by applying this formula about three to four times a week *to the scalp only*. There-after, it can be used as a scalp pack once a week.)

Another hair pack conditioner, which is often used in the best salons in Europe, is made from a simple mixture of flour and water. Rinsing it out may be a bit of work, but the results are worth the effort.

Flour Conditioning Formula
1 cup flour
1 cup water

Combine the flour and water into a paste. Apply to dry hair, and let stand fifteen to twenty minutes. Rinse thoroughly with cool water-hot water will make the paste hard to rinse out. Rinsing will probably take five to ten minutes, but you will see that your hair is much more manageable and shiny. You can shampoo and rinse after using this formula.

Molasses, which is the basis for rum, does wonders for conditioning dry hair.

Rum Conditioning Formula
3 tablespoons rum
1 egg yolk

Combine the egg yolk and rum, mixing well. After shampooing, pour the formula into your hair. Allow ten minutes for absorption. Rinse with water as cool as you can stand. Warm or hot water will poach the egg, making quite a mess.

You can really simplify this formula by applying ½ cup of blackstrap molasses to your hair and allowing it to absorb for twenty minutes. Rinse with cool or tepid water. Blackstrap molasses can be drunk as a s mineral supplement because it is rich in Calcium, Iron, Niacin, Phosphorus, Potassium, Riboflavin, Sodium—all of which you'll discover in Chapters 14 & 15 are great at promoting the health of your scalp. One caveat, though: If you choose to drink it straight from the bottle, be sure to brush your teeth immediately after, since molasses is also known for its striking capacity to promote tooth decay.

For oily hair, cantaloupe works well as a conditioner.

Cantaloupe Conditioning Formula for Oily Hair
½ cup fresh cantaloupe

Mash the melon with a fork until smooth. Massage the cantaloupe into your scalp and leave on your hair for at least 10 minutes. Rinse with cool water. As a further recommendation, you can eat the leftover cantaloupe. You'll discover in Chapter 14, what you eat has a potent significance on how you look.

3. **Scalp Packs**

As mentioned above, scalp packs are used to dry up extra sebum and absorb toxic particles from the scalp and follicles. They should only be applied to the scalp and roots with a toothbrush or pastry brush, and then the head should be covered with shower cap to utilize the body's heat in activating the chemical interaction.

Besides the modifications to the hair pack formulas noted in the preceding section, a good scalp pack can be made as follows:

Essential Scalp Pack Formula
8 ounces pure water
Herb/s of your choice
1 ounce witch hazel
½ cup Fuller's Earth

Begin by making an herbal infusion from the chart of herbs for your hair type. Bring the water to a boil, and then add one teaspoon of each of the herbs of your choice. Turn off the stove, and let the herbs steep for about 6 hours. Strain and discard the remains of the herbs. In a glass or ceramic bowl, combine the infused liquid with the witch hazel and Fuller's Earth (found at any herbal or health food store). Stir until well mixed.

Apply to the scalp and roots as described above once a week.

For people with dry or oily hair, this procedure should be utilized three to four times a week for the first four weeks of the program. Reduce the scalp pack treatment to two times a week for the next four weeks. Thereafter, a once-a-week maintenance application should be sufficient.

RINSES

Once you shampoo and condition your scalp, you will need an appropriate rinse. Rinses made from vodka, rum, or apple cider vinegar are excellent for the hair, because they work well to restore the pH balance, while softening and conditioning it. Here are the basic steps for a good rinse. Again, you can enhance the formula by adding a selection of the herbs of your choice (refer to the charts in the first half of this chapter).

Essential Rinse Formula
8 ounces pure water

Herb/s of your choice
1 ounce apple cider vinegar, rum, or vodka

Begin by making an herbal infusion from the chart of herbs. Bring the water to a boil, and then add one teaspoon of each of the herbs of your choice. Turn off the stove, and let the herbs steep for about 6 hours. Strain and discard the remains of the herbs. Stir in the vinegar or alcohol. Store in a glass jar, or squeeze bottle, and be sure to give it a vigorous shake before each use.

To use, combine one tablespoon to ¼ cup of the Essential Rinse Formula with 1 cup of warm water. Pour the formula through your hair, catching the excess in your basin. Pour again, and again. Rinse with cool water.

A good formula for stimulating hair growth can be made with nettles and lime. Both of these ingredients are renowned for their stimulating properties, which also leaves hair soft and bouncy with plenty of shine.

Lime & Nettle Rinse Formula
1 generous handful lime (or linden) flowers
1 handful of nettles
4 cups pure water
4 cups pure cider vinegar

Boil the water, and add the lime (or linden) flowers and nettles to make an infusion for ten minutes. Remove from heat and let stand for three hours. Strain the contents into a jar or squeeze bottle, while adding the cider vinegar. Let the ingredients stand for at least 24 hours before first use.

After shampooing, pour or squeeze about one cup of the rinse into your hair, soaking thoroughly. After one minute, rinse with cool water.

The above recipe has several variations depending on your particular hair quality or natural color.

Light Hair Rinse Formula
1 generous handful or chamomile flower
1 handful yarrow flowers & leaves
4 cups pure water
4 cups pure cider vinegar

Prepare an infusion by combining the flowers and leaves in boiling water. Remove from heat and let stand for three hours. Strain the contents into a jar or squeeze bottle, while adding the cider vinegar. Let the ingredients stand for at least 24 hours before first use.

Summer melon works well at restoring the natural acid protein levels in the hair shafts, while protecting oily hair.

Summer Melon Oily Hair Rinse Formula
1 orange
1 apple
1 slice honeydew melon
4 cups pure water
4 cups pure cider vinegar

Slice and peel the fruit, puncturing the orange and melon skins with a fork. Boil the fruit in pure water for ten minutes, then remove from heat and let infuse for two hours. Strain the contents into a jar or squeeze bottle, while adding the cider vinegar. Let the ingredients stand for at least 24 hours before first use.

A simplified variation of this formula with lemons is also effective for oily hair. The acids in the juice act to restore pH balance in the hair, and accentuate highlights in light or blond hair. Don't use this formula more than once or twice a week, as it will be too drying and will bleach your hair.

Lemon Rinse Formula
4 sliced lemon peels

Juice from 4 lemons
4 cups pure water

Bring the water to a boil. Add the lemon peels, cover and let simmer for ten minutes. Remove from the heat, and allow to infuse for another two hours. Strain the contents into a jar or squeeze bottle, while adding the lemon juice. Let the ingredients stand for at least forty-eight hours, and remember to give it a good shake before each use.

Southernwood has long been held in high regard for its hair growing properties, and is sometimes called "old man" because it thought to promote the growth of a new beard. Also touted for its healing properties, a simple infusion can be applied directly to the scalp to ease scalp irritations, eczema or flaking. The following formula is good for stimulating growth, or healing the scalp.

Southernwood Rinse Formula
6 heaped tablespoons southernwood
2 tablespoons sage oil
2 cups apple cider vinegar
½ cup whisky

Combine all the ingredients in a glass jar. Close and tighten the lid, then let steep for 14 days. Strain, then rebottle.

Another good formula for increasing circulation to the scalp—which promotes hair growth—is made from dried or fresh peppermint. This recipe does an excellent job of removing soap residues, while restoring the natural protein acid balance, not to mention the fact that it leaves hair smelling deliciously fresh and aromatic.

Peppermint Scalp Circulating Rinse Formula
4 heaped tablespoons dried peppermint, or
8 heaped tablespoons fresh peppermint
4 cups pure water
4 cups pure cider vinegar

Boil the peppermint in pure water for ten minutes, then remove from heat and let infuse for two hours. Strain the contents into a jar or squeeze bottle, while adding the cider vinegar. Let the ingredients stand for at least 24 hours before first use.

For people with dark, or brunette, hair, here is an excellent rinse made from rosemary and sage. The rosemary works well for promoting circulation of the blood to the scalp, while the sage acts to bring out the natural tint in darker hair, not to mention the wonderful herb scent it leaves in your hair.

Herbal Scalp Circulating Rinse Formula
2 heaped tablespoons dried rosemary
2 heaped tablespoons dried sage
4 cups pure water
½ cup pure cider vinegar

Combine the herbs in boiling water. Cover and simmer for ten minutes. Turn off the heat, and allow to infuse for an additional two hours. Strain the contents into a jar or squeeze bottle, while adding the cider vinegar. This mixture can be used immediately if desired.

For maximum effect, pour over the scalp, and allow the formula to be absorbed into the hair and scalp for approximately five minutes before towel drying.

In the chapter on shampoos, we mentioned that beer was an effective ingredient for cleansing the hair. It also works wonders as a simple rinse for restoring body and shine after shampooing.

Beer Rinse Formula
4 cups flat lager or draft beer
½ cup pure cider vinegar

Combine the beer and vinegar in a jar or squeeze bottle. Pour over the scalp and thoroughly soak the hair. Allow the formula to be absorbed for at least five minutes before towel drying. While the formula is still wet, you will smell like a pub. Don't worry. The smell disappears as the hair dries.

For extremely dry and flaky scalps, a mixture of aspirin and olive oil can resolve the problem. The aspirin does a good job of loosening the dead skin cells on the scalp, while the olive oil conditions the hair shafts.

Dry Scalp Rinse Formula
½ cup olive oil
10 aspirin tablets, finely crushed

Combine the aspirin powder with the olive oil, making sure to mix well. Store in a jar or squeeze bottle.

Thoroughly massage into the scalp for two to three minutes. Then allow to absorb for an additional five minutes before rinsing with cool water.

Styling Gels and Sprays
Styling Formulas that Add Volume to Your Hair

Most of the products you used before this program to hold and mold your hair to achieve your personal style actually are a chief factor in hair damage and loss. Many of them contain a drying isopropyl alcohol-base, which is ordinarily used as a topical anti-microbial, and should not be confused with grain alcohols derived to make rum, whiskey, or vodka. Isopropyl alcohol can weaken the protective cuticle layer of the hair shaft, as well as irritate and inflame the follicles that hold the hair to the scalp. The same is true of the "alcohol-free" products available now. The alcohol has been removed, but the damaging effects of the other chemicals haven't.

Fortunately there are several natural alternatives that you can make in your kitchen, several of which actually promote hair growth rather than the damage and loss of the store-purchased items.

Egg Setting Formula
1 tablespoon egg white
4 tablespoons tepid water

Combine the water and egg whites with a whisk until the ingredients form a smooth lotion. If you are not intending on using this immediately, store in a small jar and refrigerate. When washing your hair, remember to use cool water, or else the egg will poach on your scalp.

Sugar Spray Formula
1 tablespoon sugar
8 tablespoons warm water

Combine the sugar with the water, stirring until dissolved. Pour the formula in a spray bottle. Apply to the hair either before or after styling. This is an old, tried and true formula that works very well. Since sugar does a good job of attracting bugs and bees, it's not recommended that you use this one during the spring and summer seasons.

Unflavored gelatin combined with water is another good essential styling gel from which there are several excellent variations you can try.

Essential Gelatin Styling Formula
1 cup water
1 teaspoon unflavored gelatin

Heat the water to just before the boiling point. Add the gelatin, stirring until completely dissolved. Remove from heat and allow to cool. The mixture is ready to use when firm to the touch. If you prefer the gel to be on the stiff side, cool in the refrigerator, although this mixture is just as effective when used at room temperature. Use a small amount for styling either wet or dry hair.

Champagne, which is a combination of sugars and proteins, can be banded with the gelatin formula to thicken the hair and add more bounce.

Champagne Gelatin Styling Formula
½ cup water
½ cup champagne
1 tablespoon rosewater
1 teaspoon unflavored gelatin

Heat the water, and dissolve the gelatin as above. Add the champagne and rosewater and stir again. Pour in a wide jar, and place in the refrigerator to cool. When the formula has set, remove from the refrigerator. The mixture is ready to use when it reaches room temperature.

Almond oil added to the gelatin formula can restore hair that is damaged from the constant use of blow dryers, curling irons and rollers, while working as a very good styling gel.

Almond Oil Styling Formula
1½ cups water
1 tablespoon unflavored gelatin
1 teaspoon glycerin
1 tablespoon almond oil

Heat the water, and dissolve the gelatin as above. Add the glycerin and almond oil, stirring until well blended. Remove from heat and pour into a wide glass jar. At this point the oil will probably rise to the top. Don't worry about it; just put the formula in the refrigerator and allow to cool for one hour. Stir the formula, recombining the oil and gelatin. Return to the refrigerator for one additional hour. Remove from the refrigerator. When the formula reaches room temperature, give it one more thorough stir, then it's ready to use. This formula can be applied to either wet or dry hair to set and style.

The natural sugars in grapefruit work very well to hold the hair in place when combined with the proteins of the gelatin formula.

Grapefruit Styling Formula
½ cup water
1 tablespoon unflavored gelatin
½ cup fresh grapefruit juice
1 teaspoon glycerin
1 crushed Vitamin C tablet

Heat the water, and dissolve the gelatin as above. Add the remaining ingredients, and stir until well mixed. Pour the mixture into a wide glass jar, and refrigerate until firm (about two hours). Remove from the refrigerator. When the formula reaches room temperature, give it one final stir. It's now ready for use on either dry or wet hair.

The following is a very popular, classic kitchen recipe used down through the ages:

Volume Enhancing Styling Formula
1 cup flaxseeds
3 cups pure water
Bring the water to a boil, then stir in the flaxseeds. Reduce the heat to a simmer, then continue stirring for approximately ten to fifteen minutes. The mixture should congeal, becoming a clear gel. Remove from heat, and then strain the gel into a wide glass jar. Discard the flaxseeds.

The gel may become rather stiff, so it may be necessary to dilute it with a bit of hot water before you use it. To use, simply apply to the scalp as you would any styling gel. You'll find this works every bit as well as the expensive salon products, but it costs a mere fraction of the price. And, it's actually quite healthy for your hair and scalp.

10
Natural Hair Colorants
How to Color Your Hair Naturally Without Chemicals

Hair coloring has become as common today with men as well as women. However, the chemicals used to strip or enhance the pigmentation in the cortex of the hair shaft are extremely harsh. After repeated use to maintain your color, these chemicals will inevitably lead to serious damage. No matter what your salon stylist may say, *it will fry your hair*. Particularly if you are experiencing hair loss or thinning, and you are serious about reversing your condition and restoring your scalp to its full health, *then you must immediately stop their use*.

Fortunately, there are natural alternatives that do no damage to the hair, particularly if coloring is included as part of this program. Since you can no longer pick a shade from the side of a box, or a chart on your stylist's wall, you will need to do a sample test with many of the recipes (particularly those with henna) below to make sure you have the right color you're intending. After mixing the recipes, select a small piece of hair from the nape of your neck—a place that is usually unnoticeable. Bind the selected hair tightly with a rubber band, then apply the mixture. Wrap your hair in plastic wrap, and then let stand for the recommended time in the recipe. Rinse the sample, and dry thoroughly. Check the color under a good strong light source, such as the sun. If you're satisfied with the tint, then proceed with the whole head.

Several of the recipes require more than one application, so they do not really require a test. Simply repeat application until the desired color is achieved.

Henna has been used for thousands of years to darken hair because it is a very good semi-permanent dye that seals the cuticle layer of the hair shaft, locking in natural oils. This gives the hair enhanced shine and luster. While the color lasts as long as three to six months, it has the nice advantage of washing out gradually, so you won't see the roots develop as your hair grows.

There is one caveat to using henna: Often, when initially applied, it leaves the hair looking brassy or dull. This is completely normal, as it requires an adjustment period of about three days before your cuticles will accommodate the color. After that, it should leave your hair looking quite shiny and lustrous.

Because henna comes in several different shades, it can be mixed to produce a wide variety of tints. For instance, red henna can be combined with brown to produce auburn. Once you've determined the desired shade (and after you've tested it), you're ready for the next step:

Henna Coloring Formula
½ cup pure henna powder
   (color mixture determined from testing)
¼ cup pure water (approximate)

1. Place the henna powder in a glass or ceramic bowl. Do not use a metal bowl or utensils, as the henna may chemically react to the metal. Plastic is not recommended either, since it may permanently stain the bowl.

2. Bring the water to a boil, and then slowly add to the henna while stirring. Add only enough water until you have the consistency of mud.

    To apply, it is recommended that you use gloves to prevent staining your hands.

3. Apply the henna mixture to clean, dry hair, massaging well until the entire head is saturated to the ends of the hairs. Cover your head with a plastic shower cap.

4. To initiate the color absorption, you will need to warm your head. Sitting under a hair dryer, using a handheld blow dryer, or sitting under the sun are recommended. Continue for fifteen to forty-five minutes, depending upon how deep you want the color to be. The longer you leave it on, the darker the color will be.

5. Rinse your hair with warm water until the water is clear. Shampoo, then towel dry.

   Indigo leaves can be added to the henna paste to make a deep black tint.

   Indigo Henna Coloring Formula
   ¼ cup dark (or black) henna
   22 heaping tablespoons indigo leaves pounded
   ¼ cup pure water (approximate)
   1 egg yolk
   Corn oil

1. Combine the henna powder and indigo leaves in a glass or ceramic bowl.

2. Bring the water to a boil, and then slowly add to the henna while stirring. Add only enough water until you have the consistency of mud.

3. Allow to cool, then stir in the egg yolk.

4. Massage the scalp and hair with corn oil to prevent drying, then apply the henna mixture, massaging well

until the entire head is saturated to the ends of the hairs. Cover your head with a plastic shower cap.

Depending upon the desired shade of black in combination with your original hair color, it is recommended that you leave this on your hair for one to two hours.

5. Rinse thoroughly with cool water (you don't want scrambled egg in your hair), then shampoo and towel dry.

As listed in the chapters on shampoos, conditioners & rinses, there are several herbs that, when used repeatedly over a period of days, can produce remarkable coloring results. Ingredients like chamomile flowers, rhubarb, and mullein can lighten the hair and give it a golden sheen. Sage, tea, tobacco, can be used to darken and mask gray hair. Hibiscus flowers are used to redden hair.

Black hair:	Black henna, black malva, indigo, lavender; red henna or cloves can be added for reddish highlights
Blond or light hair:	Acacia flowers, black cherry bark, broom, calamus, chamomile, marigold, marshmallow root, orange flower, orris root, quassia chips, saffron, St. Johnswort, turmeric, yellow mullein flowers
Blue/White hair:	Bachelor button, blue malva, comfrey root, lavender (not to be used on dry hair), white chamomile flowers
Brown hair:	Aloe leaf, cassia bark, cloves, maidenhair, yarrow root
Brunette hair:	Cloves, comfrey leaf, jaborandi, lavender (not to be used on dry hair), marjoram, mint, quassia chips, raspberry, rosemary, sage, sassafras; also, herbs listed for brown or black hair
Gray/Dingy hair:	Hollyhock (turns dingy gray hair silver with bluish highlights)
Red hair:	Cloves, cochineal, marigold, red henna, red hibiscus, witch hazel bark

A basic rinse can be made with an infusion from the herbs listed above:

Herbal Coloring Rinse
¼ cup herb/s of your choice
2 cups pure water

Bring the water to a boil, then add the herb/s of your choice. Reduce heat, cover and allow to simmer for thirty minutes. Remove from heat and cool. Strain into a jar or squeeze bottle. This can be used as a rinse after shampooing and conditioning.

A coloring formula similar to the henna mixtures, which is applied to the scalp and allowed to dye the hair, can be derived from chamomile flowers.

Chamomile Coloring Formula
¼ cup chamomile flowers
2 cups pure water
8 tablespoons kaolin powder
1 egg yolk

Bring the water to a boil, then add the chamomile flowers. Reduce heat, cover and allow to simmer for thirty minutes. Remove from heat and cool. Strain, and remove half of the liquid (which may be saved for an additional application). Stir in the kaolin power and egg yolk. Apply to the hair, cover with a plastic shower cap and leave in for twenty to fifty minutes. Rinse with cool water (warm will cook the egg). This may be repeated too until the desired shade is attained.

Just like chamomile flowers, rhubarb can also be used to make a coloring formula.

Rhubarb Coloring Formula
¼ cup fresh rhubarb, finely chopped
2 cups pure water
8 tablespoons kaolin powder
1 egg yolk
½ teaspoon cider vinegar
1 teaspoon glycerin

Bring the water to a boil, then add the chopped rhubarb. Reduce heat, cover and allow to simmer for thirty minutes. Remove from heat and cool. Strain, and remove half of the liquid (which may be saved for an additional application or as the basis for the Rhubarb Lightening Rinse below). Stir in the kaolin power, then the egg yolk, cider vinegar and glycerin. Apply to the hair, cover with a plastic shower cap, and leave in for twenty to fifty minutes. Rinse with cool water (remembering that warm water will cook the egg). This may be repeated too until the desired shade is attained.

This rhubarb rinse formula can be used to reinforce the highlights obtained from the Rhubarb Coloring Formula above.

Rhubarb Lightening Rinse
¼ cup fresh rhubarb, chopped
2 cups pure water

Bring the water to a boil, then add the chopped rhubarb. Reduce heat, cover and allow to simmer for thirty minutes. Remove from heat and cool. Strain into a jar or squeeze bottle. This can be used as a rinse after shampooing.

Sage, lavender, cinnamon and tobacco are commonly used to darken hair and cover grays.

Darkening Rinse
¼ cup dried sage, or
    ¼ cup dried lavender, or
    3 cinnamon sticks
2 cups pure water

Bring the water to a boil, and then add the sage, lavender, or cinnamon. Reduce heat, cover and allow to simmer for thirty minutes. Remove from heat and cool. Strain into a jar or squeeze bottle. This can be used as a rinse after shampooing.

Sage Darkening Formula
¼ cup dried sage
2 teaspoons Lipton Tea (removed from the bags)
2 cups pure water
2 teaspoons rum

Bring the water to a boil, then add the sage and tea. Reduce heat, cover and allow to simmer for two hours. Remove from heat and cool. Strain, then stir in the rum. Pour into a jar or squeeze bottle. Apply liberally to the hair, cover with a plastic shower cap, and leave in for twenty to fifty minutes. Rinse with cool water. This should be repeated five times a week to mask premature gray hair.

Hibiscus flowers give a red highlight to light or brown hair.

Hibiscus Highlighting Rinse
Dried hibiscus flowers, or
    Hibiscus tea
Pure water

Bring the water to a boil, then add the flowers or tea. (The quantities will be determined by the amount of red highlighting that you desire.) Steep until the preferred shade appears in the water. Remove from heat and cool. Strain into a jar or squeeze bottle. This can be used as a rinse after shampooing, and may require additional applications.

11

Scalp Stimulants and Tonics

Natural Formulas to Stop Hair Loss and Stimulate Hair Growth

W e should begin this chapter with a word of caution: If you are suffering from hair thinning or loss, you may be tempted to read this chapter only and skip the rest of the book. *Don't!* While this chapter presents many recipes and formulas for stimulating hair growth, these are not in and of themselves the solution to restoring a full, healthy head of hair. The suggestions in this section represent only part of an entire, holistic program that is intended to heal more than just the symptoms, which are so painfully evident. The real solution to halting your hair loss or thinning encompasses much more than what is contained in this chapter.

There are several recipes using herbs, spices and food items that specifically are noted for their ability to penetrate the scalp and stimulate keratin production in the papilla at the base of the hair follicle.

One of the most common items is a substance called polysorbate 80. When applied to the scalp, polysorbate 80 is known to deter dihydrotestosterone (DHT) from attacking the papilla, while increasing histamine levels that stimulate hair growth.

Where does one find polysorbate 80? In mayonnaise and salad dressings, for bonding the waters and oils. Because polysorbate 80 is so readily available at every corner market, and wasn't designed and manufactured in a large pharmaceutical lab, no one has been willing to spend the millions of dollars in research required to receive approval from the FDA to officially state it has any effect on stimulating hair growth. There are no advertising agencies in New York willing to spend the tens of millions of dollars to promote polysorbate 80 to the public. Let's face it, there's more money to be made from selling a $30 tube of Rogaine than a $3 jar of salad dressing. So, why bother going after FDA approval? Even if you bought a simple tube of polysorbate 80, it wouldn't cost more than a few dollars. (At least it shouldn't. There are some disreputable companies out there who have caught on and are charging an arm and a leg for it. If you run across them, don't give them your money. Move on and go to your local health food store.)

Rosemary, nettles, chilies and cayenne peppers have all had similar success as alternatives to the expensive drug therapies described in chapter 4, and not one of them has any dangerous, or unwanted side-effects. A Basic Scalp Stimulating Formula should be applied in the morning after shampooing, then again at night before retiring. Once it is thoroughly massaged into the scalp, you should allow it to be fully absorbed, and letting it remain so it can open up the follicles and stimulate the papilla. (This formula should dry very quickly, but if you are concerned about staining your pillow, pin an old terry cloth towel over the case.)

Basic Scalp Stimulating Formula
4 ounces pure water
Herb/s of your choice
4 ounces of vodka

Begin by making an herbal infusion from the chart of herbs repeated below. Select the herbs for your particular hair type. Bring the water to a boil, and then add one teaspoon of each of the herbs of your choice. Turn off the stove, and let the herbs steep for about 6 hours. Strain and discard the remains of the herbs. Stir in the vodka, and then pour into a glass jar or squeeze bottle. Give the mixture a good shake before each application.

Massage into the scalp with the tips of your fingers, making sure to cover the entire scalp and roots. This formula will probably make your scalp tingle. Don't worry, it'll pass shortly.

Herbs and Their Properties	Normal	Dry Hair	Oily Hair
Burdock: Stimulates circulation of the scalp.	X	X	X
Chamomile: Anti-inflammatory properties; heals scalp irritations; is a natural hair tonic that also has a lightening effect, producing yellow highlights.	X	X	
Chaparral: Stimulates circulation of the scalp.	X	X	X
Comfrey: The leaves can heal irritated scalp conditions when used in an infusion.		X	
Elderflower: Anti-inflammatory properties; heals scalp irritations; gentle hair stimulant.	X	X	
Eucalyptus: Anti-inflammatory properties; heals scalp irritations; assists in regulating sebum production, and is a deep cleaning agent.			X
Garlic: Stimulates circulation of the scalp and promotes hair growth; heals scalp irritations, controls flaking, and heals eczema.	X	X	X
Horsetail: Stimulates circulation of the scalp; also a good source of silica, which promotes strength of hair shaft.	X	X	X
Indian hemp: Stimulates circulation of the scalp.	X	X	X
Lavender: Gentle hair stimulant; regulates pH levels; promotes body and shine of hair shaft; leaves a pleasant, soothing scent.	X		X
Lemon balm: Gentle cleansing herb that removes excess oil & sebum.			X
Lemon grass: Gentle cleansing herb that removes excess oil & sebum.			X
Lemon verbena: Cleanser and scalp stimulant.			X
Licorice: Contains a compound that prevents testosterone from being converted to DHT in men.	X	X	X
Marshmallow root: Has a potent conditioning and softening effect.		X	

Herbs and Their Properties	Normal	Dry Hair	Oily Hair
Nettle (a.k.a., Stinging nettle): Stimulates circulation of the scalp, and is a cleanser.	X	X	X
Parsley: Promotes the health of the sebaceous glands; heals scalp irritations; conditions, and stimulates the hair.	X	X	X
Peppermint: Stimulates circulation of the scalp; acts as a gentle antiseptic.	X		X
Red Clover: Gentle cleansing herb.		X	
Rosemary: Controls flaking and heals eczema; great for dark hair; also stimulates circulation of the scalp.	X	X	X
Sage: Helps reduce the level of sebum production in the sebaceous glands; stimulates circulation of the scalp.			X
Thyme: Cleansing & tonic properties; leaves a terrific scent.	X		X
Yarrow root: Helps reduce the level of sebum production in the sebaceous glands.			X

Exfoliating the dead cells from your scalp is a necessary step in stimulating hair growth. There are many food items when mixed with vodka that will do the job nicely:

Vodka Scalp Exfoliating Formula
4 ounces vodka
4 ounces of one of the following:
   Mashed apples, grapes, pears, strawberries, *or*
   Alfalfa, beet, ginger, or orange juice, *or*
   Beet, lavender, papaya, or pineapple extracts, *or*
   Apple cider vinegar, or Liquid chlorophyll, *or*
   Tomato puree, or
   Mustard

Combine the vodka with one selection from the list above. Apply to the scalp with a fine toothbrush or pastry brush. Allow mixture to remain on your scalp for 20 minutes, then rinse thoroughly with cool or tepid water. Repeat one to three times per week.

Special Note: Beet juice, or any other food item with strong color, should not be used on light or blond hair, as it will stain.

Bentonite, which is a type of clay mixed in water, can also be used as one of the companion ingredients in the vodka formula above. It is unusually absorbent, capable of holding over 40 times its weight. And, guess what? It specifically draws out toxins and impurities when used on the scalp. You can find it at your local health food or herbal supply stores.

With a juicer or blender, you can use fruit and vegetables to make an excellent formula for removing the dead cells and invigorating the follicles. The most effective are chlorophyll-enriched leafy green vegetables, as the chlorophyll acts as an enzyme to eat away at the unwanted skin cells:

Vegetable Stimulating Juice Formula
½ beet
½ apple (with the seeds removed)
1 stalk of celery
1 carrot
Handful of kale or spinach (organic only)

Run the ingredients through your juicer. (See Chapter 15 for more about juicing.) Apply the formula to your scalp with a soft toothbrush or pastry brush. Whatever is left over, you can drink it to clean out the insides as well. Let stand for 20 minutes, then rinse with cool or tepid water. Follow up with a shampoo and conditioner from Chapters 7 & 8.

Lecithin, brewer's yeast, and soy or whey protein compare admirably to chlorophyll-enriched vegetables as scalp stimulators.

Protein Stimulating Formula
1 scoop brewer's yeast
1 scoop lecithin powder
1 scoop soy or whey protein powder
Approx. ½ cup soy or rice milk, or pure water

Combine the brewer's yeast, lecithin, and protein powders in a glass or ceramic bowl. Slowly stir in liquid, adding only enough until blended into a pasty consistency.

Apply to the hair and scalp with a toothbrush or pastry brush. Cover with tin foil and/or a shower cap to utilize the body's heat in activating the stimulator. Leave on for 20 minutes, and then rinse with cool or tepid water. Follow up with a shampoo or conditioner from Chapters 7 & 8. Grapes, strawberries, pears, or any of the other fruits and vegetables mentioned above can be added to this recipe.

Rosemary, basil, lavender, and lemon, which are all good exfoliates in their own right, can join forces for a potent combination:

Herbal Stimulating Formula
6 teaspoons rosemary oil
3 teaspoons basil oil
3 teaspoons lavender oil
2 teaspoons lemon oil

Combine the ingredients in a small jar. An amber colored jar is preferable, as it will help to preserve the oils. Shake well to mix.

Pour two teaspoons of the formula into a small glass or ceramic bowl, and then massage the mixture into the scalp with your fingers, concentrating first on the areas that are thinning. Proceed to the rest of the scalp. Leave on overnight. The oils should be absorbed by you hair and scalp, but in case you are concerned about staining your pillowcase, use a terry cloth towel to cover the pillow. Be sure to shampoo in the morning.

A variation of the Herbal Stimulating Formula can be used once a week during the program.

Weekly Stimulating Formula
2 teaspoons Herbal Stimulating Formula
2 teaspoons basil oil (if not available, use rosemary oil)
1 teaspoon white iodine
½ teaspoon castor oil

Combine the ingredients in a small jar. An amber colored jar is preferable, as it will help to preserve the oils. Shake well to mix.

Massage into the scalp for ten minutes, starting with the areas that are thinning, then progressing to the rest of the scalp. Let stand for ten more minutes. Towel dry, and do not rinse for several hours.

Jalapeño peppers have been used in Latin American cultures for centuries to prevent hair loss and to stimulate growth.

Jalapeño Stimulating Formula
2 small or 1 large jalapeño pepper
½ cup vodka
2 tablespoons castor oil

Finely chop the jalapeño peppers and place in a glass bowl with the vodka. Cover, and then let stand for five days. Strain the vodka, and discard the peppers. Pour the vodka into a small jar with the castor oil. Seal the lid and shake vigorously before each use. Massage into the scalp in the morning, and again before going to bed. The oils from the jalapeño pepper will cause a slight tingling sensation on your scalp. It will subside in a few minutes.

Rosemary is an herb that is widely known to promote hair growth and avert hair loss.

Rosemary Stimulating Formula
2 tablespoons dried rosemary
½ cup olive oil

Combine the rosemary and olive oil in a small saucepan. Heat gently, but do not boil. Remove from heat, cover and let stand for three days. This will allow the olive oil to absorb the essential healing properties from the rosemary. Strain the oil, and discard the rosemary. Store in an amber-colored bottle. This should be massaged into the hair in the morning, and just before going to bed. Again, if you are concerned about staining the pillowcase, cover the pillow with a terry cloth towel.

This chapter could not be complete without mentioning nettles once again:

Nettles Stimulating Formula
2 cups pure water
1 heaping handful of nettle tops
2 cups white wine vinegar

Bring the water to a rolling boil. Stir in the nettle tops, cover, reduce the heat and simmer for fifteen minutes. Remove from heat. Stir in the white wine vinegar, and then let stand for one hour. Strain into a jar, discarding the nettle tops. If the scent of the nettles disagrees with you, you can add a little eau de cologne.

Massage into the hair in the morning and before retiring. As with the jalapeño pepper formula, this one will cause a slight tingling sensation on your scalp. It will subside in a few minutes.

12

Scalp Massages, Brushing, and Haircuts

Methods for Stimulating Scalp Circulation for Hair Growth

T he key to stimulating and retaining a healthful mane of hair is increasing and maintaining the quality and abundance of blood flow to the papilla in the hair follicles. If normal vasodilatation (blood flow) is obstructed, either from the genetic messages engendered in androgenetic alopecia (MPB), or stress (which causes telogen effluvium), or poor grooming habits inflaming and clogging the scalp follicles and sebaceous glands, vital nutrients and oxygen are cut off from the follicle. Without these nutrients and oxygen, the follicle dies. Hair will not grow.

There are several simple techniques you can use to directly promote circulation to the scalp and stimulate hair growth, while improving the overall condition of your scalp.

SCALP MASSAGE

A scalp massage is an effectual method for improving vasodilatation to your scalp. Since it is imperative to maintain a constant blood flow to the follicles, a massage from a licensed professional once or twice a week is insufficient to the task. Instead, a massage should be done much more frequently, at least two times a day. Of course, if you're in the position to be able to afford a masseuse two times a day, by all means indulge yourself. Otherwise, this is a very simple procedure you can administer on your own.

Begin by applying all ten fingers firmly to your scalp at the back of the neck. Without moving your fingers, push the scalp in circular motions. Keep moving and count to ten, "1… 2… 3… 4… 5… 6… 7… 8… 9… 10." Continue by repositioning your fingers and repeating by gradually moving upward and forward, covering the entire scalp. Keep repeating until you have massaged the entire scalp, including the temples, forehead and neck. With the forehead and neck, it is recommended that you utilize an upward pushing motion, rather than a circular one. Also, care should be taken when massaging problem areas that are suffering from balding or breakage—*Do not skip these areas!* Just use a little discretion. Massaging too firmly could break the remaining hairs (particularly the peach fuzz in MPB) and further damage the follicles.

This should be included as part or your daily regimen at least twice a day, once in the morning (perhaps when you shampoo) and again in the evening.

Be sure to use your fingertips. Some experts claim that using the palms of your hands is just as effective. It may be relaxing, but a flat-handed massage does not penetrate the scalp as well as the fingertips.

An alternative to using your fingers is an electric vibrator. Many of the better models come with an attachment specifically designed for scalp massage. Vibrators provide an effortless massage, and are pretty easy to use. If you have a hair loss condition, you should consider using the vibrator repeatedly throughout the day if possible. (Like the fingertip massaging technique described above, people with hair loss should use caution when working the affected areas.) If this is not practical, then at least twice a day—once in the morning and once at night—for about five to eight minutes at a time. Use the same circular motions, and upward pushing motions around the neck and forehead, as the manual massage described above.

Do not use any attachments on the vibrator, particularly hair brushes or combs. These can easily get tangled in the hair, and can be painful, besides causing breakage and possible damage to the follicles. Do not use any heat settings either, as heat will stimulate the sebaceous glands into over-activity.

The benefits of the above massage techniques will be greatly enhanced with a slant board.

SLANT BOARD

The slant board originated in India and was initially known in the West as the Yoga Slant. You can purchase one in many department and health food stores. If you should find the price prohibitive, you can easily make a homemade slant board for a fraction of the price.

Lie on the slant board with your feet at the elevated end twice a day for a maximum of ten minutes at a time. The intention here is to use the earth's gravitational pull to force your blood to your scalp, increasing vasodilatation and feeding the papilla in your follicles.

To augment the value of your time spent on the slant board, you can apply a scalp massage. Begin with a finger massage for approximately five minutes, and then conclude with a vibrator massage for an additional five minutes.

If you happen to own a back swing, or gravity boots (recommended only for the very fit), these can be used instead of the slant board. If you have a condition of high blood pressure, then you need to consult your physician who will most likely advise you to stick to using the slant board.

Be sure to use caution when standing, as the increased level of blood suddenly draining from your head can cause dizziness.

BRUSHES

Before we talk about brushing, lets take a look at your brush. Take a few moments, set this book down, and go to your bathroom to retrieve your brush. While you're at it, grab your comb. Don't forget the ones in your briefcase, or purse as well.

Take a look at them. Now, ask yourself 'When was the last time I washed this?' If you're like most people, you can't remember.

Think about this: Every time you washed your hair to get it clean, you probably used your brush or comb to style it afterwards—the dirty brush or comb you're holding right now. Think about this, as well: Isn't it a lot like taking a shower and putting on dirty clothes again?

All that collected dirt and oil just goes back onto your hair and scalp, effectively re-clogging the pores and follicles you just cleansed with shampoo. You need to clean your brushes and combs *every day that you use them*. This can be done in the shower while you shampoo, since shampoo is the best product to clean them with. Shampoo is designed to remove the oils and dirt that collect on the scalp, and it works just as well on your brush.

Administer a small amount of shampoo on the bristles, and work it into the brush. Run your comb through the bristles to loosen the dirt and oils. Rinse in hot water, and then repeat until thoroughly clean. Give it a good shake to release the excess water, then dry on a soft cloth towel. After the initial cleaning, it should be quite easy to maintain if practiced on a daily basis.

If you have no interest in taking the time to clean your brush, then you can wrap it in cheesecloth. The cheesecloth will not interfere with the bristles, and will collect the grime and oils from your hair. The cloth should be changed daily.

There are many types of brushes available, but the best kind is made from boar's hair. You can find this type at any beauty supply store or salon. The bristles are very similar to the keratin of human hair and absorb oil and dirt just like your hairs do. Nylon brushes do not work anywhere near as effectively as boar's hair, and are not recommended. Another benefit of natural bristles is that the tips of the bristles are rounded, which is gentler on the scalp and hair shafts. Nylon bristles are usually sharp, and can lead to follicle inflammation and hair breakage.

Brushes and combs should be replaced at least once a year. Eventually the bristles will weaken and break, which leads to split ends and breakage.

BRUSHING

Never use a brush when your hair is damp. Hair expands when it comes into contact with water, essentially weakening the outer cuticle layer and making the shaft noticeably brittle. The hair become so elastic when wet that brushing could easily stretch the shafts to the breaking point. Use a wide-toothed comb with rounded teeth.

A regimen of brushing (when your hair is dry) is a critical part of preventing hair loss and nurturing the vitality of your hair. The gentle pulling from brushing stimulates vasodilatation to the scalp. It encourages the proper functioning of the tiny erector pili muscles to squeeze the sebaceous glands, which lubricates the hair with sebum, promoting a more lustrous, healthy condition. Additionally, brushing removes dead cells from the epidermis, dirt, and any remaining waxy buildup.

To succeed at stimulating the scalp, you must brush twice a day, once in the morning and again in the evening. Gently brush for three to five minutes (three minutes for short hair, or five minutes for longer). If you bend your head to the floor, you will increase the amount of blood, which will maximize the benefits of brushing. Brush from the neck forward to the front of the scalp, then from the sides to the crown of the scalp. Lastly, brush from the front of the scalp toward the neck.

If your hair has tangles, work them out delicately from the ends.

HAIRCUTS

Most people visit their salon or barber about every two to three months. On this program, you will need to go once a month. This may seem excessive, but there are two very good reasons: First, your hair will be growing much faster; you'll *need* to go. Second, cutting the dead, or split, ends helps keep the hair and scalp healthy. The more you cut those split ends, the healthier your hair will grow. But, if those new hairs don't have the room to grow, *they won't*.

The method used to relieve the pressure from these new hairs is very simple. You can take this book along with you for your stylist or barber and they can easily follow the instructions. Methodically sectioning the hair horizontally and snipping the ends of each section, then vertically re-sectioning for cutting will give the hair lift and provide plenty of room for the new hairs to grow. Be sure that the peach fuzz hairs on thinning or balding spots get snipped, too. This will also assist in the growth of new hairs in these regions, too.

13
Skincare and the Face
Healthy Hair Comes with Healthy Skin

How you care for your face is a critical, and often disregarded, aspect in the overall health of your hair, and a determining factor in hair loss. This is particularly so for men, who are content to wash with a bar of soap and give it a shave once a day, not really paying much attention at all to the condition of the epidermis on their face. Poor skincare promotes a buildup of sebum. This is the waxy oil that the sebaceous glands use to lubricate hair, and is the same oil that causes pimples and blackheads on the face.

A buildup of sebum on the face and forehead traps dead skin cells. Instead of falling away from the epidermis, as they're supposed to do, they act to clog the pores. Up near the hairline, this discourages the proper functioning of the follicles, and advances the conditions of damage and alopecia.

Regular hand and body soap should never be used to clean the face. The pH balance in these soaps strips away the necessary oils that are intended to lubricate a healthy face, and many of these soaps have antibacterial formulas that remove both the good and bad bacteria. Read the label on the soap: It ain't called *hand* or *body* soap for nothing.

A good facial routine has three basic steps applied both in the morning and evening: Cleansing, Toning, and Moisturizing. Men should not worry: This won't take but just a couple additional minutes in the bathroom, and the results will be absolutely worth it. Not only will the well-being of your hair improve, but also the texture of your face will appear more vibrant and healthy.

Women are strongly urged not to skip over this part of the program. Most of you already have your favorite line of products you've relied on for years. Set them aside and try the formulas in this chapter. There are two particular advantages over using these recipes: First, they don't have any harsh chemicals (isopropyl alcohol and witch hazel, which are very drying and are No-No's) that can build up over time and damage your face. If you're using something from the drug store, you probably are doing more harm than good. If you're using a line of products from your favorite department store, then you're probably being gravely overcharged. The second advantage is that you won't be paying for any expensive advertising, or licensing fees for the use of a famous designer's name on the label.

CLEANSING

Using a cleanser will dislodge any dirt, grime, or oils collected in the pores. Oatmeal is a popular and exceptional natural cleanser. It's very mild and soothing, and is good for sensitive skin.

> **Oatmeal Cleansing Formula**
> ½ cup oatmeal
> 1 cup pure water
> 1 teaspoon glycerin
> 1-2 drops tincture of benzoin

Combine all of the ingredients in a food processor or blender. Puree into a creamy, smooth paste. Store in an airtight jar, or plastic container.

To use, apply a small amount to the face, gently scrubbing in circular motions over the cheeks, forehead and nose. Make sure you reach all the way up to the hairline. Rinse well with warm water and pat dry.

A simpler formula can be made from combining three of the most effective cleansing grains.

3-Grain Cleansing Formula
½ cup cornmeal
½ cup oatmeal
½ cup wheat germ

Stir the grains together, and then store in an airtight jar or plastic container.

To use, combine two teaspoons of the formula with just enough water to create a paste. Massage over your face, gently scrubbing in circular motions. Rinse well with warm water and pat dry.

Cleanser for Dry Skin
Yellow of an egg
1 tsp. Almond oil
1 tsp. Honey

Gently warm honey and almond oil. Stir into the egg yolk. Apply over face and leave for ten minutes. Rinse with warm water and then with cool water.

Cleanser for Oily Skin
1 Tbsp. Yogurt
1 Tbsp. Buttermilk
4 oz Herbal infusion
    (rosemary, lavender, lemon balm)
    use separately or combine.

Pour into a jar and store in the refrigerator. Use morning and night to cleanse your face.

Lemon juice is a natural astringent that does a good job of removing dirt and oil, while correcting and restoring the skin's essential acid level. When combined with yogurt and sunflower oil, it can cleanse as well as moisturize.

Lemon Yogurt Astringent Formula
1 tablespoon fresh lemon juice
1 tablespoon sunflower oil
½ cup plain yogurt

Combine the ingredients in a glass bowl and mix well. Store in a jar and keep in the refrigerator.

To use, pour a small amount onto your hand, then massage over your face, gently scrubbing in circular motions. Rinse well with warm water and pat dry.

Mint combined with apple cider vinegar does a very good job of improving complexions with enlarged or coarse pores.

Apple-Mint Astringent Formula
3 tablespoons fresh mint
6 tablespoons apple cider vinegar
2 cups pure water

Chop the mint and combine with the vinegar in a glass jar. Screw on the lid and let stand for one week. Strain the vinegar through a layer of cheesecloth, and discard the mint. Add the water to the vinegar, and shake well before each use. This can also be stored in a squeeze bottle.

During the summer when you're cleaning strawberries, save the leaves from the tops of the fruit. They have four times as much Vitamin C in them than oranges, which is very good for invigorating the skin.

Strawberry Astringent Formula

½ cup fresh strawberry leaves
¼ cup apple cider vinegar
¼ cup rosewater

Combine the strawberry leaves and vinegar in a jar. Screw on the lid and let stand over night. Strain the vinegar, and discard the leaves. Add the rosewater and shake well to mix before each use. Store in a jar or squeeze bottle.

Astringents are good at removing residue sebum and dirt, while opening the pores and preparing them for the second toning step. They can be applied to the face with your bare fingers, white cotton balls, or pure white facial tissues. Do not use toilet paper, or facial tissues with color or patterns. The dyes and perfumes in these products can cause skin irritation.

TONING

Using a toner will remove any remaining dirt and dead cells that may clog the pores, and they act as a humectant that prepares the skin for the third step, moisturizing. Toners should be applied with a white cotton ball, or pure white facial tissue using gentle circular motions on the skin. Be sure to apply it at the top of the forehead, just below the hairline.

Apple-Mint Toning Formula

3 tablespoons fresh mint leaves
2 tablespoons apple cider vinegar
1 cup pure water

Chop the leaves until fine. Combine all of the ingredients in a jar. Screw on the lid and let stand for three days. Strain the formula through a layer of cheesecloth, and discard the mint leaves. Store in a clean jar, or squeeze bottle. Shake to mix well before each use.

Honey is particularly good for healing blemishes and softening the skin.

Honey Toning Formula
1 tablespoon honey
1 teaspoon fresh lemon juice
1 tablespoon rosewater
2 tablespoons apple cider vinegar

Combine the ingredients in a jar or squeeze bottle. Shake until mixed before each use. To prevent the formula from feeling sticky, allow it to sit in the refrigerator for five days. If you don't want to wait that long, rinse your face with cool water after application.

Chamomile flowers are frequently used in cosmetics because they relieve inflammation and work to assist the skin in absorbing moisture.

Chamomile Toning Formula
3 Chamomile tea bags (100% chamomile only)
2 cups pure water
1-2 drops tincture of benzoin

Bring the water to a boil, and pour over the tea bags in a ceramic or glass heat-resistant bowl. Let steep for several hours until cool. Remove the tea bags, then stir in the tincture of benzoin. Store in a jar or squeeze bottle.

MOISTURIZING

The process of cleansing and toning is beneficial because you are removing the sebum and dirt that clog your pores (which can lead to hair loss and damage). It also strips away the H_2O, which is necessary to keep your skin healthy and vibrant. Keeping the skin moist is the crucial third step to subduing and balancing the oil production of the sebaceous glands.

Basic Moisturizing Formula
¼ cup mineral oil
¼ cup stearic acid powder
½ teaspoon baking powder
2 tablespoons glycerin
1 cup pure water

Combine the mineral oil and stearic acid in a microwave-safe bowl.

Combine the remaining ingredients in a second microwave-safe bowl.

Heat the mineral oil and stearic acid on High until the powder has melted, and the mixture is clear, stirring occasionally.

Heat the water, baking powder and glycerin in the microwave until it just starts boiling (about two minutes on High). Slowly stir the water into the oil solution. It will foam to twice its volume, as carbon dioxide is released from the powder.

Pour the mixture into a blender and blend on High for two minutes, or until the mixture turns white and has a fluffy consistency. Spoon into a clean bowl and let stand until cool. Stir once again, then spoon into a jar for storage.

To use, massage a small amount onto your face and neck.

A modified version of this formula uses coconut oil, which is extremely nourishing for the skin.

Coconut Moisturizing Formula
¼ cup coconut oil
¼ cup stearic acid powder
½ teaspoon baking powder
½ cup pure water

Combine the coconut oil and stearic acid in a microwave-safe bowl, and heat on High until melted.

Combine the baking powder and water in a second microwave-safe bowl. Stir until the powder is dissolved. Heat in the microwave until it just starts boiling (about two minutes on High). Slowly stir the water and baking powder into the oil solution. It will foam to twice its volume, as carbon dioxide is released from the powder. Stir thoroughly. Let stand until cool. Stir once again, then spoon into a jar for storage.

To use, massage a small amount onto your face and neck.

Cornstarch can be used to make a formula that works wonders for severely dry or chapped skin.

Cornstarch Moisturizing Formula
4 tablespoons cornstarch
4 tablespoons glycerin
4 tablespoons rose water
1 cup pure water

Combine all of the ingredients in a microwave-safe bowl and stir until thoroughly mixed. Heat on High (stirring every 30 seconds) until boiling and the mixture turns thick. Remove from the microwave and let stand until cool. Spoon into a jar for storage.

Should this jelly-like formula thicken over time, just stir in one tablespoon of water at a time until the formula thins enough to use.

Honey can be used to make a very simple moisturizing formula.

Honey Moisturizing Formula
2 tablespoons honey
24 drops almond oil

Combine the ingredients in a glass or ceramic bowl. Whip the oil and honey until they are completely mixed. Pour into a small jar, and store in the refrigerator.

To use, apply a tiny amount to each cheek and forehead. Massage gently, working in circular motions up toward the hairline. (Make certain you don't get this in your hair.) Use sparingly.

Eye, Lips, Throat lift
1 oz apricot oil
1 oz almond oil
1 oz avocado oil
1 oz wheat germ oil

Put all oils together in an amber glass bottle with a screw top. Shake thoroughly. Apply around eyes, mouth and neck at bedtime. The oils will sink into the skin and plump out the lines.

These three steps—cleansing, toning and moisturizing—constitute a daily routine that will promote skin care, and prevent hair loss and damage.

Now, there is one more step to caring for your face that you will need to do once a week:

MASKS

A once-a-week mask will be very beneficial. It will help to unclog the pores of your face, remove dead cells and any remaining oil or other impurities, heal blemishes, and replace lost moisture while soothing the skin.

An added benefit to having a weekly mask is the fact that it requires you to relax, to remain calm and quiet for twenty to thirty minutes. Once a week, you are guaranteed to have half an hour to let everything go and pamper yourself. As you'll see later, having time to be alone, to meditate, or to simply reduce the stress in your life is an important factor in reversing hair loss and damage.

Once again, oatmeal makes a good cleanser, and because it is rich in protein and nutrients like magnesium, iron, potassium, and phosphate, it's nourishing for the skin. Select one of the following formulas for your skin type:

Oatmeal Mask Formula for Normal Skin
½ cup cooked oatmeal
1 tablespoon almond oil
1 egg

Oatmeal Mask Formula for Dry Skin
½ cup cooked oatmeal
½ banana, mashed
1 tablespoon honey
1 egg yolk

Oatmeal Mask Formula for Oily Skin
½ cup cooked oatmeal
½ cup apple, mashed
1 tablespoon fresh lemon juice
1 egg white

Combine all of the ingredients in a bowl and mix until a smooth paste is formed.

To use, apply to the face, and let stand for about twenty minutes. Rinse with tepid water. Pat dry, then apply a moisturizing formula derived from the aforementioned recipes.

Brewer's yeast is rich with vitamins, and is an excellent source for the proteins your skin requires. It comes in either a powder or in tablets, and can be found at most health food stores and many larger super markets.

Brewer's Yeast Mask Formula
1 teaspoon powdered brewer's yeast, or
6 tablets of brewer's yeast, crushed
1 tablespoon buttermilk or plain yogurt

Combine the ingredients in a bowl and mix together until smooth. Store in the refrigerator

Apply evenly to the face, and leave until dry, about twenty minutes. Rinse with tepid water. Pat dry, then apply a moisturizing formula derived from the aforementioned recipes.

Clay does a terrific job of drawing out trace impurities and sebum, while refining the texture of your skin. The following is a classic formula that has been used for centuries.

Clay Mask Formula
1 tablespoon clay powder
2-3 tablespoons pure water

Mix together the clay and water in a ceramic bowl, adding only one teaspoon of water at a time until a smooth paste forms.

Apply the formula to your face, covering all areas except the eyes. Allow the clay to dry for about 20 to 30 minutes. Rinse with warm water. When the mask has been removed, rinse with cool water to close the pores. Pat dry, then apply a moisturizing formula derived from the aforementioned recipes.

This formula can be used as a mask, as well as a conditioning formula for your hair:

Egg & Oil Mask Formula
1 egg
1 teaspoon salt
1¼ cup vegetable oil
½ cup apple cider vinegar

Combine in a blender or food processor the egg, salt, and ¼-cup vegetable oil. Turn the blender on medium, then slowly add another ¼-cup vegetable oil. Slowly add ¼-cup of the cider vinegar. After that, slowly add another ¼-cup vegetable oil, then the remaining cider vinegar. Then, add the final ¼-cup vegetable oil in a slow steady stream. The ingredients should now form a creamy, white mayonnaise that can also be used as a delicious sandwich spread.

To use, apply to the face and let stand for about twenty minutes. Rinse with tepid water. Pat dry, then apply a moisturizing formula derived from the aforementioned recipes.

14

From the Inside Out: You Are What You Eat

Nature's Way to Beautiful Hair and Vibrant Health

Just like the nails on your toes and fingers, and the skin cells on the outer most layer of your epidermis, the hair you see on your scalp is fundamentally dead tissue. However, the follicle structure imbedded in the second and third layers of the epidermis is very much alive and is intricately dependent on the circulation of the blood through the body. Without a proper balance of nutrients, minerals, proteins, essential fatty acids, and trace minerals, the papilla will not properly synthesize proteins into keratin and produce healthy hair cells. Accordingly, the resulting hair growth will be less than optimal.

Clinical studies have shown a strong connection to hair loss with deficiencies in the class of B-Complex vitamins. While it may appear to be an issue that could not possibly affect western cultures due to the overabundance of food available, nothing could be further from the truth. Whole grains such as rice and wheat, while organically rich in B-Complex, are commonly processed before they reach the market shelf. Consequently, they are stripped of many of their vital nutrients. The prevailing practice in most western households of over-steaming vegetables removes many of the B vitamins since they are water-soluble. The emphasis on fast and processed foods in the modern diet often supplants the intake of raw leafy greens, another superior source of B's. This is further complicated by the fact that our western diet is heavy with white flour, sugar and refined grains. So that our bodies can digest these refined carbohydrates, the B's that we do manage to ingest often get redirected to supporting their assimilation rather than nourishing our bodies.

Nicotine, caffeine, grain alcohol and sugar are common stimulants that work like a two-edged sword affecting hair loss and the vitality of your hair. As they move through your system, they devour nutrients that are missing from their chemical structures. They also overwork the adrenal glands, eventually depleting them and increasing the nutritional requirements of your body. Most significantly, this raises the androgen levels in the bloodstream. As we saw in Chapter 3, androgens are the hormones that convert the enzyme 5-alpha reductase into DHT. DHT restricts vasodilatation to the papilla, eventually leading to hair loss.

Animal products—such as milk, butter, fatty meats and cheese—are very common in our western diets. These foods increase the levels of cholesterol, which is synthesized in the liver to produce steroidal hormones. High cholesterol in the bloodstream virtually translates into high levels of DHT as well.

Our western diet is also low in fiber, which means that foods abide in our systems longer than they should. The food ferments as a result of increased bacteria, augmenting the toxicity levels in the bloodstream, and further inhibiting the optimal absorption of nutrients. The bottom line is that the hair follicles rely on the nutrients they receive from the blood. Insufficient quantities of fiber are another key factor in inhibiting hair growth.

With the understanding that hair is 97% protein, it is easy to see how insufficient levels of protein intake can also be a contributing component in hair loss and poor hair health. Strict vegetarians, vegans, people on severe weight-loss regimens, and those suffering from eating disorders (i.e., anorexia nervosa, and bulimia) do not ingest an adequate daily supply of protein. Hair loss usually begins within two to three months as the follicles in the growth cycle shift into the dormant telogen state in a defensive attempt to conserve protein levels.

Before you jump to the conclusion that increasing protein levels to high amounts will prevent hair loss, you should know that eating too much protein will cause the same problems as eating too little. If protein intake exceeds 15 to 20% of your diet, your body will go into a kind of 'negative mineral balance' and react virtually the same as when protein levels are inadequate. Daily protein intake should never exceed more than 30 to 40 grams.

Studies have also linked salt intake to hair loss. Sodium from common table salt is retained in the tissues of the scalp (and throughout the body), hampering their functions.

A nutritionally balanced diet will not be of much benefit if the body is incapable of transmuting the elements it requires. As we get older, the body is less and less able to absorb nutrients. This is initially indicated by the fact that the stomach fails to produce as much acid as it did earlier in life, evidenced by the increased presence of gas, heartburn, and bloating. Sensations of exhaustion after a meal tend to point to the digestion process also burning up too much energy.

Protein, which is the building block of hair, is usually the first victim of poor digestion.

Proper digestion involves four principal stages, and begins in the mouth with the production of saliva. Saliva launches the digestive course by breaking down carbohydrates and preparing food for peristalsis, the journey through the digestive tract. The secretion of stomach acids is activated by the chewing action.

The second stage happens in the stomach with the secretion of enzymes from the pancreas. These enzymes break down the food, and are replaced from enzymes found *only* in raw foods. Since the quintessential western diet accentuates cooked foods over raw, the pancreas is frequently unable to secrete adequate levels of enzymes by middle age, and requires the assistance of an enzyme supplement. Ironically, while a supplement will assist the pancreas, it will also weaken it by making it dependent on the supplement.

The third stage involves the secretion of hydrochloric acid to further the breakdown of food. Heartburn results from an insufficient level of this acid.

When the food is almost completely digested, it passes from the stomach into the intestines. Stage four involves the bacteria acidophilus, which plays a large part in enzyme production and conveys nutrients into the bloodstream. Acidophilus also supports the immune system, coordinates oscillations in hormone levels, controls the amounts of cholesterol, and is a preventative factor in cancer of the colon.

Unfortunately, acidophilus is easily annihilated by many factors in our diet and culture. Chlorinated tap water, food poisoning, and smoking are just to name a few. Antibiotics, which are intended to kill bacteria, act haphazard in their task, killing the helpful acidophilus bacteria without differentiation. Insufficient levels of acidophilus give rise to harmful bacteria, essentially poisoning the bloodstream. Classic symptoms of low acidophilus levels include increased flatulence, gas, halitosis (bad breath), acne, indigestion, and headaches. (Food products such as yogurt, miso and sourdough do contain acidophilus, but in such insufficient levels that they fail to have any restorative function. Concentrated acidophilus in the refrigerator section of your supermarket or health food store is the only thing that will rebuild this bacterium in your system.)

The high fat/high protein composition of most western diets leads to a buildup of fatty deposits along the walls of the intestinal tract, effectively preventing the absorption of nutrients into the bloodstream. As the buildup continues over time and the body becomes increasingly deprived of vitamins and minerals, the feeling of satisfaction after a meal becomes more and more difficult to achieve.

To discharge this buildup, an increase of fiber is necessary. Psyllium husks do the trick quite well, and are commonly found in such commercial products as Metamucil. Psyllium husks inflate with water and scour the intestinal walls, pushing out old matter. Since it will also indiscriminately remove bacteria, an acidophilus supplement should be taken along with psyllium husks. A cleansing program of one level tablespoon of psyllium husks mixed with six ounces of water (accompanied by another six ounces of water with acidophilus) twice daily can be implemented for up to ten days. Thereafter, once or twice a week should be ample.

Vitamins in adequate measures are absolutely indispensable to maintaining the health of the body. The condition and quantity of hair on the scalp is a direct reflection of that vitality. While it is outside the range of this book to be the definitive guide on the general well-being of the body, it is pertinent to look at the vitamins and minerals that are closely connected to preventing hair loss, stimulating growth, and engendering healthy hair. You should keep in mind that your nutritional requirements will be particular to your age, weight and height, diet, etc. It is recommended that you consult a nutritional specialist or your physician before taking a trip to the health food store to buy up an inventory of supplements. We will also be suggesting dietary changes that should more than adequately meet your needs.

Vitamin A is essential for strong bones, sharp eyes, healthy glands, skin, teeth and hair. When combined with zinc and silica, it assists in the proper functioning of the sebaceous glands. Vitamin A deficiencies can lead to a clogging of the sebaceous glands and a thickening of the scalp, which symptomatically leads to flaking, and a buildup of sebum in the pores. With the pores closed off, the follicles cannot breath, and hair cannot grow.

Smoking, air pollution, aspirin products, antibiotics, laxatives, barbiturates and certain cholesterol-lowering drugs can work to deplete the body of Vitamin A. 10,000 I.U. per day is considered a safe supplemental dosage for most adults. This vitamin is fat soluble, which means the body stores whatever it doesn't immediately use in fat cells (unlike B & C vitamins, which are water-soluble with the excess being eliminated through urine). Too high of a dosage of Vitamin A can inflame the hair follicles, so it's very important not to overdo it.

Foods that are rich in Vitamin A:

Alfalfa	Celery	Rose hips
Apricots	Fish liver oils	Sweet potatoes
Beets	Green & Red Peppers	Spinach (organic)
Broccoli	Liver	Tomatoes
Cabbage	Kale	Yellow squash
Cantaloupe	Oranges	Watercress
Carrots	Parsley	

A good general rule of thumb to follow is, if it's a yellow or green fruit and vegetable, then it's probably high in Vitamin A.

The B-Complex of vitamins has gained a lot of notoriety for its ability to impact the health of hair. It should be noted that the B's are interconnected and depend upon one another to have any useful effect on the body. While a number of specific B's play a significant role in the health and growth of your hair, you should always take a B-Complex. You can, of course, augment the intake of particular B's known to stimulate hair growth and vitality, but they should never be taken on their own. They just won't work without the entire B-Complex family.

Foods that are rich in B-Complex:

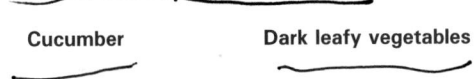

Cucumber	Dark leafy vegetables

One of those B's, Biotin, has particularly been touted for its preventative properties in hair loss. It works as a coenzyme that aids in the proper absorption of carbohydrates, fats and proteins, supports cell growth, the assimilation of essential fatty acids, and assists the body in the employment of other B-Vitamins. Biotin has a high sulfur content, which is a mineral the body uses as a primary cleansing agent, and is an indispensable component for stimulating hair growth. Sulfur comprises about .25 percent of the body, and can be found in every cell, with the highest concentrations found in hair, skin and nails. It detoxifies the blood, and protects against radiation and pollution. Sulfur is a key component of the protein structure keratin, which comprises 97 percent of the hair shaft.

Biotin has also shown considerable evidence that, when used topically with Niacin (a form of B-3 that releases histamines), it does promote hair growth.

Grain alcohol, antibiotics and egg whites are known to nullify Biotin. A good supplemental dosage is about 300 micro-grams, but should be taken with a B-Complex to promote absorption and balance the body's usage of the B's.

Foods that are rich in Biotin:

Brewer's yeast	Kidney	Poultry
Brown rice	Lettuce	Seafood
Cauliflower	Liver	Soybeans
Egg yolk	Mushrooms	Spinach (organic)
Grapefruit	Nutritional yeast	

Foods that are rich in Sulfur:

Brussel sprouts	Dried beans	Fish
Cabbage	Egg yolk	Turnips

Niacin, a form of Vitamin B-3, works wonders in stimulating blood circulation. At a dosage of about 100 mg, Niacin taken on its own (which is the only exception in the B-Complex family) will release histamines in the body, flushing blood to the capillaries throughout the skin, including the scalp. If you've never taken a Niacin supplement, you should know that the release of histamines will cause a distinct tingling sensation, and your skin will temporarily turn red with a slight rash. This is completely normal and is harmless. Additionally, the release of histamines will also discharge Heparin, a substance which is essential for cell growth and is intimately connected to the papilla's production of hair cells.

Niacin is also marketed in a formula with 200 micro-grams of Chromium, which is intended for lowering cholesterol and does not have the tingling side effect. Do not buy this version, as it is only possible to obtain the histamine-releasing properties when Niacin is taken on its own. Because of this, we will disregard the listing of foods that are rich in B-3.

There are two members of the B-Complex family that specifically work as antioxidants and as cell membrane stabilizers: Inositol, and Para-aminobenzoic acid (commonly known as PABA). These two vitamins have a shielding action on the hair follicles by protecting them from membrane damage promoted by oxidized cholesterol collecting in the scalp.

PABA behaves as a coenzyme, assisting in breaking down proteins in the blood stream and utilizing them efficiently. It is also a key-supporting factor in the healthy production of red blood cells. Studies with daily doses of 1,000 to 3,000 mg have indicated that PABA does retard hair loss and reverses premature graying of the hair stemming from nutritional deficiencies and stress. It is usually recommended in doses of 100 mg in a healthy dietary regimen.

Foods that are rich in PABA:

Cabbage	Nutritional yeast	Sunflower seeds
Eggs	Oats	Whole grains
Mushrooms	Spinach (organic)	

By linking with choline to form lecithin, Inositol stimulates a healthful stream of nutrients and blood flowing to the hair follicles and scalp region. Similar to PABA, studies have demonstrated that Inositol is connected to the prevention of hair loss and premature graying. Because of its link to the formation of lecithin, it also works at metabolizing cholesterol and fats, and prevents narrowing and hardening of the arteries. Inositol is also noted for its sedative effects, and can be used to alleviate mild cases of hypertension by lowering blood pressure. In cases of hair loss related to stress, Inositol plays a major role in treatment. Symptoms of an Inositol deficiency, besides hair loss, include abnormalities of the eyes, eczema, constipation, and insomnia. Those who drink black tea, coffee and sodas with caffeine should be aware that caffeine depletes the body of Inositol, and should therefore consider cutting back on your consumption and/or take a supplement. Recommended daily doses range from 100 to 200 mg in your dietary regimen.

Foods that are rich in Inositol:

Beets	Lecithin	Oranges
Cabbage	Legumes	Tomatoes
Cauliflower	Nutritional yeast	Unrefined molasses
Citrus fruits	Onions	Whole grains
Kale		

Far more notable for its anti-stress properties than Inositol is B-5, Pantothenic Acid. In fact, B-5 has gained so much credibility for stress reduction, that it is commonly marketed as the primary ingredient in anti-stress vitamin formulas. B-5 also plays a primary part in producing adrenal hormones, and it is an essential vitamin in the output of antibodies. It also serves the body in assimilating many other vitamins, and the efficient metabolizing of proteins, fats, and carbohydrates. Symptoms of B-5 deficiency can include hypoglycemia, fatigue, irritability, skin problems, premature aging, as well as hair loss and premature graying. Pantothenic acid has also been used in the treatment of depression and some anxiety disorders. Remarkably, there is evidence that this vitamin also extends life expectancy, having demonstrated a 20% increase in the life expectancy of lab mice, while augmenting endurance and stamina. For hair loss prevention, recommended daily supplemental dosages are 100 mg taken three times daily.

Foods that are rich in B-5:

Beans	Fresh vegetables	Royal jelly
Bee Pollen	Grapefruit	Salt-water fish
Cauliflower	L-Cysteine (see below)	Strawberries
Eggs	Oranges	

L-Cysteine is an amino acid that comprises approximately 8% of hair, and is commonly included as a component in many hair growth vitamin supplements. It works to preserve and protect cells by combating harmful toxins in the blood stream. High doses of L-Cysteine can reverse the positive effects of this amino acid, and can lead to bladder or kidney stones. When taking L-Cysteine, it is strongly recommended that three times as much Vitamin C be ingested along with it, since Vitamin C counteracts the toxic effects of high levels of L-Cysteine. A hair growth regimen should include 500 mg of L-Cysteine accompanied by at least 1,500 mg of Vitamin C two times per day.

Foods that are rich in L-Cysteine:

Alfalfa	Cauliflower	Horseradish
Apples	Currants	Kale
Beets	Filberts	Legumes
Brussel sprouts	Garlic	Onions
Cabbage	Hazelnuts	Pineapples
Carrots		

Vitamins C and E are also critical to hair growth. Vitamin C performs a wide multitude of functions throughout the body. It is a significant factor in the formation of collagen, is obligatory for proper adrenal gland functions (indispensable in managing stress levels), and encourages healthy circulation to the scalp. Recommended daily dosages for hair growth range from 500 to 3,000 mg in a time-released formula. Check to make sure that the Vitamin C supplement you purchase includes Bioflavinoids, which are a co-factor for the proper absorption of Vitamin C and work to reinforce the capillaries and veins all through the blood stream (including the ones feeding the papilla in your scalp).

Foods that are rich in C:

Black currants	Green peppers	Rose hips
Cabbage	Kale	Spinach (organic)
Citrus fruits	Parsley	

Increasing oxygen uptake to the blood stream is of vital necessity to improving circulation in the scalp, and this is the role of Vitamin E. Deficiencies in Vitamin E are indicated by brittle, dull hair shafts, as well as hair loss. A hair growth program should include between 400 I.U. to 800 I.U. of natural Vitamin E. (Avoid the synthetic versions derived from petroleum, as the body does have a problem absorbing it, and eventually blocks it at the E receptor sites.)

Foods that are rich in E:

Cold-pressed vegetable oils, especially wheat germ oil

Here's a summary table of the vitamins discussed above, and their co-factors, showing the foods they can be found in:

Vitamins	Foods
A:	(Occurs in nature only as carotene, which is converted in the body to Vitamin A.) Alfalfa, apricots, beets, broccoli, cantaloupe, carrots, cabbage, celery, fish liver oils, green & red peppers, kale, liver, parsley, oranges & rose hips, spinach, sweet potatoes, tomatoes, yellow squash, watercress
B-Complex:	Cucumber, dark leafy vegetables
B-1:	Beet tops, beets, carrots, dandelion, grapefruit, spinach
B-2:	Beet tops, carrots, celery, green peppers, kale, parsley, spinach, turnip greens
B-3 (Niacin):	Asparagus, kale, parsley, potatoes
B-5:	Beans, bee pollen, cabbage, cauliflower, eggs, fresh vegetables, grapefruit, oranges, royal jelly, salt water fish, strawberries
B-6:	Carrots, lemons, pears, potatoes, spinach
Folic Acid:	Carrots, oranges, parsley, potatoes, spinach

Vitamins	Foods
Biotin:	Brewer's yeast, brown rice, cauliflower, egg yolk, grapefruit, kidney, lettuce, liver, mushrooms, nutritional yeast, poultry, seafood, soybeans spinach
PABA:	Cabbage, eggs, mushrooms, nutritional yeast, oats, spinach, sunflower seeds, whole grains
Inositol:	Beets, cabbage, cauliflower, citrus fruits, kale, lecithin, legumes, nutritional yeast, onions, oranges, tomatoes, unrefined molasses, whole grains
C:	Black currants, cabbage, citrus fruits, green peppers, kale, parsley, rose hips, spinach
L-Cysteine:	Alfalfa, apples, beets, Brussel sprouts, cabbage, carrots, cauliflower, currants, filberts, garlic, hazelnuts, horseradish, kale, legumes, onions, pineapples

Along with the vitamins listed above, there are a number of essential minerals that are required for your hair's roots to take in proper nourishment: Iodine, Zinc (especially for men), Sulfur (which we've discussed above), Potassium, Iron, and Silica.

Iodine regulates the thyroid gland, encouraging the hormone Thyroxin. Thyroxin metabolizes and conveys nutrients to the millions of blood vessels, nerve endings, and lymph vessels throughout the body, as well as all of the sebaceous glands in your scalp. Thyroxin passes through the subcutaneous layer of fat just under the scalp and feeds the hair follicles, inducing the sebaceous glands to secrete sebum. The most effective iodine supplement available is made from sea kelp and other ocean plants. This form of iodine is chemically indistinguishable from the form located in the thyroid gland. It is also recommended that you switch from common iodized table salt to non-iodized sea salt. Iodized table salt is a synthetic form of iodine, which builds up in the body and eventually overwhelms the thyroid.

Zinc deficiencies can also inhibit the hormonal functions of the thyroid. It should be noted that most American men are Zinc deficient. Deficiencies are often linked to having too much Copper in your environment, especially hot water plumbing, cookware, or some contraceptive devices for women. Studies have shown that Zinc improves the body's ability to utilize Vitamin A. Since these two work so well together, it is logical that your program should include both. 3 mg of Copper should also be taken, as it supports the body's metabolic absorption of Zinc.

Recommended daily Zinc dosages range from 15 mg to 50 mg. However, taking too much Zinc can also inhibit the thyroid. Since each body has different needs, you must be careful when taking a Zinc supplement. Zinc cannot be tasted when the body is deficient, but it has a distinct metallic taste when enough has been absorbed. Purchase a non-flavored Zinc lozenge with a low potency of about 5 mg per tablet. Keep track of how many lozenges you ingest by starting with three 5 mg tablets, and gradually increase the amount over a few days. At some point you will notice the taste change, and that means you've exceeded your maximum. Zinc is stored in the body, so reduce your intake a bit over the next few days until the metallic flavor has disappeared. At that point, you need to begin increasing the dosage again.

Foods that are rich in Zinc:

Egg yolks	Nutritional yeast	Soybeans
Fish	Oats	Spinach (steamed)
Legumes	Pumpkin seeds	Sunflower seeds
Mushrooms	Seafood (especially oysters)	Tomatoes (raw)

Potassium promotes optimal muscle contraction, and, along with sodium, balances the levels of water retained by the body. (Diuretic drugs and caffeine can easily deplete Potassium.) Potassium also plays a role in distributing nutrients throughout the body and is quintessential in hormonal secretions. Symptoms of Potassium deficiency include persistent fatigue, dull, lackluster hair, eczema, itchy scalp, and a condition in which the hair oscillates from being extremely oily to being extremely dry.

Foods that are rich in Potassium:

Avocados	Kale	Parsley
Bananas	Lemons	Potatoes
Celery	Molasses	Spinach
Dried fruits	Nutritional yeast	Tangerines
Grapes	Nuts	Yams

Symptoms of a low-grade Iron deficiency include dry, brittle hair, as well as fatigue, and rough, chapped skin. Full-blown anemia is often indicated by hair loss. If you suspect that you have anemia, or may be Iron deficient, *it is strongly recommended that you consult with your doctor.* When purchasing an Iron supplement, avoid the common type called Ferrous Sulfate. It is remarkably difficult for the body to assimilate, often building up deposits in the liver and eventually leading to serious liver problems. Before taking an Iron supplement, you should try correcting the deficiency by adjusting your diet.

Foods that are rich in Iron:

Almonds	Eggs	Molasses
Beets	Fish	Poultry
Dates	Green leafy vegetables	Raisins
Dried prunes	Kidney & Lima beans	Whole grains

Oxygen is the most abundant element on the earth's crust. Silicon is the second, and is encountered chiefly in the form of Silica. Silica promotes cell metabolism and production, controlling the aging process. It maintains and restores our eyes, teeth, nails, skin and hair. A Silica supplement should only be purchased if it has been processed as an "organic vegetal Silica from aqueous extract." Unprocessed Silica usually is sold in the herb horsetail. Ingesting unprocessed horsetail can have extremely toxic side effects, particularly on the prostate gland in men. Recommended daily dosages of an aqueous Silica extract supplement range from 10 to 20 mg. For hair restoration, daily dosages should be increased to levels between 30 and 60 mg for up to one month.

Foods that are rich in Silica:

Asparagus	Leeks	Rhubarb
Cabbage	Lettuce	Rice, Rice, Rice
Cauliflower	Oats	Strawberries
Celery	Onions	Sunflower seeds
Cucumber	Parsnip	Swiss chard

Another interesting note about Silica is that it is found in exceptional amounts in nettles, which is a factor that accounts for this plant's restorative properties in hair. Organic vegetal Silica can be purchased in a powder form and added to any of the shampoo recipes in Chapter 7. (There are a few commercial shampoos available that include Silica as an ingredient, but the amount is insufficient to have any effect; it's not much more than a clever ploy from the manufacturer's marketing department.)

Here's a summary table of the minerals discussed above, and some of their co-factors, showing the foods they can be found in:

Minerals	Fruit & Vegetables
Calcium:	Cabbage, carrots, elderberries, kale, lemons, mustard greens, tangerines, turnip, watercress
Iron:	Almonds, beets, dates, dried prunes, eggs, fish, green leafy vegetables, kidney & lima beans, molasses, poultry, raisins, whole grains
Magnesium:	Beets, elderberries, endive, lemons, raspberries
Phosphorous:	Beet tops, cabbage, carrots, grapes, kale, raspberries, spinach, tangerines, watercress
Potassium:	Celery, dandelions, grapes, kale, lemons, parsley, potatoes, spinach, tangerines, and most leafy green vegetables
Silica:	Asparagus, cabbage, cauliflower, celery, cucumber, leeks, lettuce, oats, onions, parsnip, rhubarb, rice, strawberries, sunflower seeds, Swiss chard
Sodium:	Beets, carrots, celery, cherries, dandelions, kale, peaches, tomatoes
Sulfur:	Brussel sprouts, cabbage, dried beans, egg yolk, fish, turnips
Zinc:	Egg yolks, fish, legumes, mushrooms, nutritional yeast, oats, pumpkin seeds, seafood (especially oysters), soybeans, spinach, sunflower seeds, tomatoes (raw)

When most of us think of supplements, we think only of vitamins and minerals. But, we're missing out on a vital third class known as Essential Fatty Acids (EFA's). EFA's assist in maintaining the well-being of the body, mind and emotions, and are considered essential for your diet because they are not naturally produced in the body. Low level deficiencies are indicated by dry, brittle hair, hair loss, and skin (which also includes the scalp) conditions of dryness, flaking, itching or psoriasis. Advanced occurrences of EFA deficiencies include symptoms of confusion, fatigue, general weakness, bruising, pain and inflammation in the joints. There is also convincing evidence in recent medical studies that EFA deficiencies lead to a swelling of the sebaceous glands, giving rise to excessive secretions of sebum. In turn, this incites clogging of the follicles, malnutrition of the hair root, and increased hormone levels of 5-alpha reductase (which is converted into DHT, restricts vasodilatation to the papilla, and advances hair loss).

Supplemental sources of EFA are available in cod liver oil, wheat germ oil, evening primrose oil, and flaxseed oil. Avoid taking cod liver oil, since the amount required for any therapeutic benefit is so great that you will run a grave risk of overdosing on Vitamins A and D.

Evening primrose and flaxseed oils are available in capsule and liquid forms. They each have slightly different fatty acids, so they should both be included in your daily regimen. Normal dosages should be three capsules, or one tablespoon of each per day. For hair growth and restoration, the amounts should be doubled to six capsules, or two tablespoons of each per day. Since these fatty acids lack certain co-factors required to derive their benefits, you must take them along with a good multi-vitamin and mineral supplement. Make sure the following nutrients are included: Biotin, Niacin, B-6, C, E and Zinc.

High levels of saturated fats found in vegetable and animal products work against EFA's, so avoid taking these supplements with meals prepared using those fats. Additional things to avoid, or which could hinder the body's absorption of EFA's, are high cholesterol levels, immoderate alcohol consumption, diabetes, repeated viral infections, and nutritional deficiencies. Unavoidably, old age also hinders the assimilation of EFA's. Consuming polyunsaturated fatty acids (hydrogenated vegetable oils, e.g. margarine and deep fried foods) will also stop EFA's in their tracks. (Polyunsaturated fatty acids are a chief ingredient in the formation of free radicals in the body, and should be avoided at all costs. Free radicals are now commonly believed to be the mechanism responsible for premature aging, problems with the immune system and cancer.)

Because of this, it is highly recommended that you refrain from cooking with vegetable oils, shortening, and animal fats. Replace them with monounsaturated fats such as olive, canola, and peanut oils. These oils do not interfere with EFA's, nor do they promote free radicals. Your palate may need to adjust to the tastes produced from cooking with these oils, but they are lighter and allow for the true flavors of the foods to come through in their preparation.

An excellent source for EFA's is deep-sea fish such as salmon, mackerel, trout, herring, or sardines. Two or three meals a week including one of these fish should provide an adequate supply of EFA's.

There are a number of herbs that are known for their ability to improve the condition of the scalp and promote hair growth. One of which, nettles, has already been mentioned repeatedly through this book. An extract derived from nettle root has been successfully shown to inhibit the activity of 5-alpha reductase, as well as bolstering the endocrine glands. (In men, nettle root extract also works as a decongestive on the prostate gland, relieving discomfort from conditions of enlargement.)

Saw Palmetto has gained an even more substantial reputation than that of nettles. An extract derived from Serenoa Repens (Saw Palmetto berries) is effective at blocking the conversion of testosterone into DHT, and also prevents DHT's ability to lock onto cellular receptor sites. A recommended dose of Saw Palmetto extract is 160 mg taken twice a day.

Foenum-graecum, commonly known as Fenugreek, is a plant widely used for a variety of medicinal applications. The seeds are very nourishing, and are customarily administered to convalescing patients to encourage weight gain, especially those suffering from anorexia nervosa. Fenugreek also helps to inhibit cancer of the liver, lower blood cholesterol levels, and is used as an anti-diabetic. It works in combination with thyme as a strong mucilage that cleans the mucous from the body, maximizing the metabolic synthesis of vitamins, minerals, EFA's and other herbs, making it indispensable for a hair growth or restoration program. Crushed seeds can also be mixed with olive oil and massaged into the hair to give it a glossy sheen.

Here's a table of other herbs and plants that are effective in the care of your hair. Take this list to your local herbal supply or health food store and ask your supplier to recommend the best brands and combinations available:

Eczema:	Burdock, cade, germander, lycopodium powder, moss, pansy, pine tar, thyme, violet, white willow bark
Hair conditioning:	Basil oil, cherry bark, lavender oil, nettle & cherry bark, ragwort, rosemary
Dark hair:	Bergamot, clove, creosote, jaborandi, nettle, rosemary, sage, southernwood
Dry hair:	Acacia, chamomile, clover, comfrey root, cowslip, elder flower, melitot, orange flower, peach leaf
Hair growth:	American bearsfoot, astralgus root, butcher's brood, ginger & horseradish, gingko biloba leaves, jaborandi, marshmallow root, rhubarb root, rosemary, sea kelp, shave grass, southernwood, spirulina, uva ursi
Hair loss:	Ginger & horseradish, gobernadora, rosemary, shave grass, southernwood, spirulina
Light hair:	Chamomile, comfrey root, cowslip flower, elder flower, marigold, orris root, quassia chip, white willow bark
Oily hair:	Bergamot, lemon grass, orris root, quassia chip, strawberry, white willow bark, witch hazel bark
Psoriasis:	Birch bark, chamomile, cajuput, comfrey root, germander, lecithin, pansy, papaya, sea kelp, thyme, white willow bark, wintergreen

SUPPLEMENT SUMMARY

For your convenience, here is a summary listing of the major points in this chapter, with all the vitamins, minerals and EFA's described, as well as others that work in concert with them. Take this list to your local health food store, and read the labels on the supplement bottles. If you have any questions, talk to the person behind the counter. You will be surprised to find how well informed they are. Western culture has begun to acknowledge the healing powers of herbs and other supplements, and the people who work in health food stores have had to become highly proficient in the subtleties of how these supplements work.

Protein Intake: 30 to 40 grams per day (or 15 to 20% of your diet)

Psyllium Husks: (always taken with an acidophilus supplement)

Cleansing Program: 1 level tablespoon mixed in 6 ounces of water, and an acidophilus supplement with an additional 6 ounces of water twice daily for up to 10 days.

Maintenance Program: 1 level tablespoon mixed in 6 ounces of water, and an acidophilus supplement with an additional 6 ounces of water twice a week.

VITAMINS:

- Vitamin A: 10,000 I.U. per day
- A good B-Complex should include the following:
- B-3 (Niacin in a B-Complex supplement): 50 mg 3 times per day
- B-3 (Niacin by itself without Chromium or any other supplements): For stimulation of hair growth, take 100 mg once daily.
- B-5: 100 mg 3 times per day.
- B-6: 50 mg 3 times per day
- Biotin: 100 micro-grams 3 times per day.
- Folic Acid: 100 micro-grams 3 times per day.
- Inositol: 100 to 200 mg per day.
- PABA: 100 mg per day (For Hair Loss: 1,000 to 3,000 mg per day).

- L-Cysteine: 500 mg twice per day with 1,500 mg of Vitamin C at each dosage.
- Vitamin E (natural only; avoid petroleum derived versions): 400 to 800 I.U. per day.

MINERALS:

- Copper: 3 mg per day
- Iodine: 150 micro-grams per day
- Iron: Use only with a doctor's supervision.
- Sea Kelp: 500 mg per day
- Potassium: 200 mg per day
- Selenium: 30 micro-grams per day
- Silica: Purchase only versions derived as "organic vegetal silica from aqueous extract"; take 10 to 20 mg daily; for hair growth stimulation, increase to between 30 and 40 mg per day.
- Zinc: Use 5 mg lozenges ranging between 15 to 50 mg daily, depending upon the presence of a metallic taste.

ESSENTIAL FATTY ACIDS (EFA's):

- Evening Primrose Oil & Flaxseed Oil: 3 capsules or 1 tablespoon of each once per day; for hair growth stimulation, take 6 capsules or 2 tablespoons of each once per day.

HAIR GROWTH & RESTORATION DIET

A lot of options and information have so far been included in this chapter. It might be helpful for you to tie it all together with a suggested diet that will revitalize your body and stimulate the growth and luster of your hair. This diet really should be considered more as a guideline than something to be used as a strict regimen to punish yourself with. As long as you stick with the foods mentioned in this chapter, and follow the principles in Chapter 15, you will find that you have a lot of room to switch the menus around so you don't get bored.

Here are a few things to remember when making food choices:

1. Drink water, lots of water—at least 8 ounces an hour.

2. Cut down on the caffeine intake; if not, remove it altogether.

3. If you must use a sweetener for your coffee, tea, or just about anything else, try to use a substitute. At the very least, use brown or raw sugar.

4. Cut down on your intake of table salt, preferably cutting it out all together.

5. Start out your program with a psyllium husk cleanser, twice a day for the first seven to ten days. Thereafter, take a maintenance dose once or twice a week. You can mix it in with your juicing formulas, which are described in Chapter 15. Remember to take an acidophilus supplement to restore those critical enzymes.

6. Stick to fresh foods. Steam your vegetables for no more than five minutes. Refrain from processed or refined products, particularly jellies and sweets.

7. Remove any fat and skins from all meats before preparing.

8. If you take vitamin supplements, take them at the end of the meal, unless the instructions specifically say otherwise.

9. Cut out the polyunsaturated fats, like vegetable oils, margarine, and animal fats from your diet. Cook with monounsaturated fats such as olive, canola and peanut oils. These oils do not interfere with EFA's, nor do they promote free radicals.

10. If you're a vegetarian, or wish to cut back on your intake of meats, you will need to get your protein from other sources. Combining certain food groups in your recipes and cooking will optimize your selections:

   * Grains (cereals, corn, pasta, or rice) should be combined with Legumes (Beans, lentils, or peas).

   * Grains should be combined with Dairy Products such as cheese, and milk.

   * Seeds (sesame, or sunflower) can be combined with Legumes.

11. Pull out your recipe books, get creative, and have fun! Cooking can relieve a lot of stress, and promotes a positive sense of well-being by you allowing yourself the freedom to be creative. There are a few recipes following the diet to get you started.

Here a suggested menu for your first seven days:

Sunday

Breakfast
Zinc Juice Formula
  (See end of Chapter 15)

Mid-morning snack
A juice formula of your choice
  (See Chapter 15)

Lunch
½ Cantaloupe
1 cup low-fat yogurt
Roasted chicken breast

Mid-afternoon snack
A juice formula of your choice

Dinner
Salad with dark leafy greens & lettuce with light olive oil, mustard, or raspberry vinaigrette dressing
Broccoli Beef (see recipe below)
Watercress Restoration Juice Formula (See end of Chapter 15)

Desert (if desired)
Fresh fruit cocktail

Monday

Breakfast

Stimulating Ginger Juice Formula
  (See end of Chapter 15)

Mid-morning snack

A juice formula of your choice

Lunch

Tuna on spinach greens & tomato
slices with light olive oil dressing

Milk, or Soy Milk

Mid-afternoon snack

A juice formula of your choice

Dinner

Salad with dark leafy greens &
lettuce with light olive oil, mustard,
or raspberry vinaigrette dressing

Chicken Provencal
  (see recipe below)

Berries with low-fat yogurt

Desert (if desired)

Baked apple

Tuesday

Breakfast

Potent Potassium Juice Formula
  (See end of Chapter 15)

Mid-morning snack

A juice formula of your choice

Lunch

Tomato soup with brown rice

Whole grain crackers with natural
peanut butter

Citrus fruit

Milk, or Soy Milk

Mid-afternoon snack

A juice formula of your choice

Dinner

Salad with dark leafy greens &
lettuce with light olive oil, mustard,
or raspberry vinaigrette dressing

Broiled salmon

Steamed rice

Zesty Zinc Juice Formula (See end of
Chapter 15)

Desert (if desired)

Fresh fruit cocktail

Wednesday

Breakfast

Zinc Juice Formula

Mid-morning snack

A juice formula of your choice

Lunch

Fresh fruit salad on a bed of dark leafy greens

1 cup low-fat yogurt

Orange juice

Mid-afternoon snack

A juice formula of your choice

Dinner

Vegetable soup

Whole grain crackers

Salad with dark leafy greens & lettuce with light olive oil, mustard or raspberry vinaigrette dressing

Broiled steak

Rice pilaf

Desert (if desired)

Fresh fruit cocktail

Thursday

Breakfast

Stimulating Ginger Juice Formula

Mid-morning snack

A juice formula of your choice

Lunch

Tuna fish on whole grain bread

Fresh citrus fruit

Milk

Mid-afternoon snack

A juice formula of your choice

Dinner

Salad with dark leafy greens & lettuce with light olive oil, mustard or raspberry vinaigrette dressing

Chicken Italiano (see recipe below)

Zesty Zinc Juice Formula

Desert (if desired)

Fresh fruit laced with
  Vanilla Rice Dream

Friday

Breakfast

Potent Potassium Juice Formula

Mid-morning snack

A juice formula of your choice

Lunch

Vegetable soup with brown rice

Pineapple slices

Low-fat yogurt with a banana

Orange juice

Mid-afternoon snack

A juice formula of your choice

Dinner

Lentil-Barley soup

Whole grain crackers

Salad with dark leafy greens & lettuce with light olive oil, mustard or raspberry vinaigrette dressing

Roasted Turkey with Rosemary & Sage

Steamed broccoli

Desert (if desired)

Fresh fruit cocktail

Saturday

Breakfast

Stimulating Ginger Juice Formula

Mid-morning snack

A juice formula of your choice

Lunch

Cottage Cheese Leek Salad (see recipe below)

Fruit

Orange juice

Mid-afternoon snack

A juice formula of your choice

Dinner

Mushroom soup

Salad with dark leafy greens & lettuce with light olive oil, mustard or raspberry vinaigrette dressing

Sesame Chicken (see recipe below)

Watercress Restoration Juice Formula

Desert (if desired)

Fresh melon slices

A FEW SUGGESTED RECIPES

Green Leafy Herbal Salad
1 Garlic clove
Romaine Lettuce
Organic Spinach Leaves
Dandelion leaves
Nettle leaves
Endive
Parsley, minced
Watercress
Green peppers, sliced
Tomatoes, sliced
Sprigs of marjoram, mint, tarragon, thyme

Begin by rubbing your salad bowl with clove of garlic. Then toss together the greens, parsley, and watercress. Arrange the green peppers and tomatoes over the greens. Place small sprigs of any of the herbs over the top. Combine lemon juice and olive oil for a simple dressing. Pour over salad, then toss the ingredients lightly before serving.

Green Salad
Organic spinach
Watercress
Parsley
Romaine
Beet tops
Dandelion tops
Celery tops
Carrot tops
Green pepper
Endive

You can select any three of the items above, or all of them if you wish. You can add any other greens you can find, and they'll probably taste pretty good. This is particularly delicious when served with French dressing.

Cottage Cheese Leek Salad
1 Leek
1 cup cottage cheese
Sunflower seeds
Red pepper

Chop the leek finely, and mix with cottage cheese. Sprinkle with sunflower seeds, and garnish with red pepper slices.

Broccoli Beef
1 pound top sirloin steak, sliced thin
2 carrots, sliced ¼" thick
2 red bell peppers, sliced
1 clove garlic, minced
1 large onion, sliced
1 cup broccoli flowerets
¾ cup beef broth
1 teaspoon ginger
¼ teaspoon cinnamon
3 tablespoons cornstarch
1 tablespoon of pure water
dash of red pepper flakes
dash of soy sauce
dash of hot pepper sauce
2 cups steamed rice

Dredge beef in 2 tablespoons of cornstarch. Heat a pan with olive oil for sautéing. Add ginger, then meat and cook until brown. Remove from pan. Add and stir-fry onions, garlic, carrots, and bell pepper. Add broth, seasonings, and hot sauce. Bring to a boil and add broccoli. Cook until tender. In a separate bowl, combine remaining tablespoon of cornstarch and water. Add to vegetable mix, stirring until well blended. Stir in beef and cook until thick. Serve over rice.

Makes 4 Servings.

Chicken Provencal
2 large chicken breast halves,
   sliced into nuggets (remove the skins)
2 onions, chopped
2 cloves of garlic, minced
½ cup red wine
1½ cup tomatoes, sliced
16 black olives, sliced
dash of rosemary
dash of thyme
dash of salt
dash of coarse black pepper
dash of Worcestershire sauce
½ pound fresh green beans, cut up

Brown chicken nuggets and remove. Add garlic and onions. Add wine and simmer until reduced to ¼ cup. Return chicken. Add tomatoes, olives, seasonings, Worcestershire sauce, and green beans. Simmer until chicken is done. Can be served over pasta or steamed rice.

Makes 4 Servings.

Chicken Italiano
2 large chicken breasts
2 onions chopped
1 garlic clove, minced
dash of ginger
½ teaspoon paprika
½ teaspoon cumin
½ teaspoon oregano
¼ teaspoon turmeric
dash of cayenne
1½ cups chicken broth
1 cup fresh tomatoes, sliced
1 cup garbanzo beans
1 large zucchini, sliced

dash parsley
1 tablespoon lemon juice
2 cups pasta, cooked

Sauté chicken and remove. Sauté onions and garlic. Add seasonings and cook for 30 seconds. Add broth, tomatoes, and chicken. Heat through. Add zucchini and garbanzo beans. Heat through. Add parsley and lemon juice. Serve over pasta.

Makes 4 servings.

Sesame Chicken
1 pound chicken breast halves, sliced thin
  (remove the skins)
1 roasted red pepper for each chicken breast
1 cup scallions, finely chopped
1 garlic clove for each chicken breast, minced
1 pound snow peas
2 tablespoons sesame seeds, roasted
½ cup teriyaki sauce
8 ounces steamed rice, or rice noodles, cooked

Marinade chicken in teriyaki sauce over night. Sauté garlic and peppers, then remove. Add chicken and cook until no longer pink. Add peppers and snow peas. Heat through. Add scallions and sesame seeds. Then serve over noodles or rice.

Makes 4 Servings.

15

Food for the Follicle:
Freshly Squeezed Juice
Vitamins and Minerals to Feed the Root of Your Hair

When the nutrition and health food movement started a few decades ago, the literature available overflowed with information about the effect vitamins and minerals had toward reversing alopecia and restoring the health of the hair. When that movement began, the neighborhood drug stores were devoid of the myriad supplements available today. Research showed that the most potent manner for providing the body with nutrients was obtainable through the juicing of organic fruits and vegetables. The body effortlessly assimilates juices due to the fact that they are high in enzymes that help in the digestion process. Not only that, but unused enzymes are stored in the body and later used to help digest cooked foods, almost entirely lacking in these enzymes. Since enzymes can deteriorate quickly, juices must be made fresh and consumed while fresh. The nutrients and materials break down quickly as well, which means that most juices purchased in a store have lost much of their alimentary value. The pasteurization process, which is meant to prolong shelf life, completely dissolves the chemical structure of enzymes.

Plants inherently drink up the minerals and nutrients available in the soil, and, in short, are the most potent source for these life-giving constituents. Juice—which is comprised of water, flavors, pigments, enzymes, vitamins, minerals, and nutrients—works synergistically to furnish your body with the materials that promote healing, provide energy, and optimize the functions of the glands, organs and tissues, including the scalp and hair.

Since the intent of juicing is to supply the papilla in the scalp with nutrients via the bloodstream, the most commonly prescribed vegetable is carrot. Carrot juice contains most of the minerals essential for the body, and is rich in iron, potassium, silica, and sulfur. Its alkaline balancing properties in the bloodstream work to strengthen the nervous system, and stimulates the endocrine glands to secrete hormones required by the hair roots.

Cucumber and lettuce enhance carrot juice, because they are so high in silica and sulfur. Cucumber also contains Vitamin A, B-Complex, C, Calcium, Manganese, Phosphorous, Potassium, and Sodium. The Sodium content in cucumber and lettuce maintains the Calcium, keeping it in a fixed solution until the body utilizes it.

Nettles (there's that plant again!) are highly advantageous when added to juices, because they are remarkably saturated with Iron, Potassium, and Silica, while also being abundant in Vitamins A and C, Iron, and Sulfur.

Spinach juice is also regularly recommended for hair restoration and growth, often in combination with either lettuce or carrot. Spinach carries two caveats, though: It contains high levels of oxalic acid, and should be avoided by people with kidney stones in their medical history. (The same is true of rhubarb.) Non-organic spinach is also ignominiously recognized for its ability to trap and hold pesticides.

Healthy hair growth is at least partially contingent upon the sulfur-enriched amino acids. And so, it is no wonder that the Roman Empire believed watercress was a good cure for hair loss, since it is the vegetable with the highest Sulfur content next to horseradish. It also contains Vitamins A, C, B-1, Folic Acid, Biotin, B-3, Pantothenic Acid, as well as Calcium, Iron, Potassium, Sodium, and Zinc. It is one of the very best sources of Iodine. Watercress has an extremely strong flavor, so it recommended that a handful be juiced with four or five carrots, a bit of parsley, a stalk or two of celery, and perhaps some dark green lettuce. (The combination of spinach and watercress is considered to be awfully overpowering, so it is not recommended.)

High in protein, alfalfa—the plant, not alfalfa sprouts—was first acclaimed by the Arabs, who named it "Al Falfa," which translates as "The Father of All Foods." Its nutrient composition is so abundant due to the fact that its roots dig down about thirty feet below the surface, extracting minerals that are unapproachable by most other plants. Permeated with Vitamins A, Biotin, Inositol, PABA, C, D, and E, it also contains striking ratios of Calcium, Iron, Magnesium, Phosphorous, Potassium, Silica, as well as Sulfur. Its high chlorophyll content assists in the detoxification of the bloodstream and builds red blood cells. Additionally, alfalfa is a source of eight enzymes, which work to metabolize and assimilate nutrients. It can be purchased as a supplement tablet in most health food stores, and should be taken in doses of six to ten tablets per day.

Below is a table listing the vitamins with the fruits and vegetables they can be found in:

Vitamins	Fruit & Vegetables
A:	(Occurs in nature only as carotene, which is converted in the body to Vitamin A.) Alfalfa, apricots, beets, broccoli, cantaloupe, carrots, cabbage, celery, fish liver oils, green & red peppers, kale, liver, parsley, oranges & rose hips, spinach, sweet potatoes, tomatoes, yellow squash, watercress
B-1:	Beet tops, beets, carrots, dandelion, grapefruit, spinach
B-2:	Beet tops, carrots, celery, green peppers, kale, parsley, spinach, turnip greens
B-3 (Niacin):	Asparagus, kale, parsley, potatoes
B-5:	Beans, bee pollen, cabbage, cauliflower, eggs, fresh vegetables, grapefruit, oranges, royal jelly, salt water fish, strawberries
B-6:	Carrots, lemons, pears, potatoes, spinach
Folic Acid:	Carrots, oranges, parsley, potatoes, spinach

Vitamins	Fruit & Vegetables
Folic Acid:	Carrots, oranges, parsley, potatoes, spinach
Biotin:	Brewer's yeast, brown rice, cauliflower, egg yolk, grapefruit, kidney, lettuce, liver, mushrooms, nutritional yeast, poultry, seafood, soybeans spinach
Inositol:	Beets, cabbage, cauliflower, citrus fruits, kale, lecithin, legumes, nutritional yeast, onions, oranges, tomatoes, unrefined molasses, whole grains
C:	Black currants, cabbage, citrus fruits, green peppers, kale, parsley, rose hips, spinach
E:	Cold-pressed vegetable oils, especially wheat germ

Below is a table listing the minerals with the fruits and vegetables they can be found in:

Minerals	Fruit & Vegetables
Calcium:	Cabbage, carrots, elderberries, kale, lemons, mustard greens, tangerines, turnip, watercress
Magnesium:	Beets, elderberries, endive, lemons, raspberries
Phosphorous:	Beet tops, cabbage, carrots, grapes, kale, raspberries, spinach, tangerines, watercress
Potassium:	Celery, dandelions, grapes, kale, lemons, parsley, potatoes, spinach, tangerines, and most leafy green vegetables
Sodium:	Beets, carrots, celery, cherries, dandelions, kale, peaches, tomatoes

Below is a table listing the minerals with the fruits and vegetables they can be found in:

Trace Elements	Fruit & Vegetables
Copper:	Asparagus, black & red currants, kale, potatoes
Iodine:	Oranges, spinach
Manganese:	Apricots, green lettuce, kale, oranges, spinach
Zinc:	Apples, asparagus, carrots, kale, lettuce, pears, spinach, tomatoes

It's relatively easy to make fresh juices. All you need is a good juicer (available in most appliance stores and super-marts), and high-quality produce. The following tips will help you to prepare juices that are both delicious and effectual for your hair program:

- Whenever possible, use organic produce. When organic produce is unavailable, consider peeling your fruits and vegetables to remove any trace pesticides.
- Wash your produce before juicing. Take care to remove moldy or bruised portions.
- Do not use the skins of oranges and grapefruits, as they contain substances that can be toxic when consumed in large quantities over time.
- Kiwi, papaya, and other tropical fruits should be peeled as well, since they were most likely grown in countries where carcinogenic pesticides are still legal.
- All pits and apple seeds, which contain cyanide, should be removed. (The seeds of lemons, limes, melons, and grapes are perfectly fine.)
- Do not use carrot or rhubarb greens, as they are toxic. The leaves and stems of most other produce are fine. However, the leaves of celery are pretty bitter, so they aren't recommended either.
- Most produce should be sliced or chunked to accommodate the size of your particular juicer.
- Produce with low water content cannot be juiced, so don't use them: Bananas and avocados are good examples of what not to juice.
- A good serving size is about six to eight ounces. To receive the most nutritional value, make your juices just before drinking them. Juicing too far in advance will break down the enzymes, and other nutrients.

Below are a few suggested formulas of fruits and vegetables particularly effectual for stimulating growth and restoring vitality to the hair. Feel free to play around with them by adding your own ingredients, or by mixing them up. And remember, if you don't feel like drinking the whole serving, save some and massage it into your hair!

Basic Hair Growth Juice Formula
2 dark green lettuce leaves
Handful of alfalfa
4-5 carrots

Watercress Restoration Juice Formula
Handful of watercress
½ handful parsley
4-5 carrots
2 stalks of celery
½ cup fennel, chopped
½ apple

Stimulating Ginger Juice Formula
¼ inch slice ginger root
½ apple
4-5 carrots

Potent Potassium Juice Formula
Handful parsley
Handful spinach
Handful of alfalfa
2 stalks of celery
4-5 carrots

Zinc Juice Formula
1 nectarine
1 cup plain low-fat yogurt
¼ cup orange juice
2 tablespoons wheat germ, or
   1 tablespoon psyllium husks

Zesty Zinc Juice Formula
1 tomato
2 large carrots
1 teaspoon grated lemon zest
1 cup plain low-fat yogurt

16

Exercise and Other Ways to Jumpstart the Circulation

Techniques for Stimulating Blood to the Root of the Hair

Increasing the flow of oxygen to the blood stream is a primary goal in any hair growth and restoration program. Exercise is another important component in achieving that goal. It should be an essential part of anyone's lifestyle, not merely because of its widely recognized benefits—weight control, improved cardiovascular fitness, increased strength, protection against diabetes, and an improved sense of well-being—but, with regards to the subject at hand, you should be aware that exercise, or the lack of it, has a significant impact on the adrenal system throughout the body. In short, the adrenal glands and hormonal secretions of a sedentary person do not function as optimally as do those of someone who exercises regularly. Another benefit is the fact that vigorous exercise will also release hormonal eicosanoids, which dilate the blood vessels and increase the flow of oxygen to the capillaries (including those feeding the follicles in the scalp).

What is more, the vitamins, minerals and EFA's described in the previous chapters can't be absorbed properly in the bloodstream without exercise. Instead, a large percentage of them get rerouted and stored in the adipose tissues, or fat cells (unless they are water soluble, like the B's and Vitamin C, in which case they are more likely flushed out of the system during urination).

Clearly the goals of increasing the flow of oxygen to the blood stream and decreasing the body's fat content are of paramount concern to someone seeking to stimulate hair growth or restore the vitality of your hair.

Now, before you sigh that groan of resignation ("Oh, no! You mean I have to go to the gym?"), this chapter will show you several easy ways to add exercise into your daily routine. Many of these suggestions can be done from home with a minimal impact on your schedule. And, research has shown that it doesn't require too much effort to gain the benefits of working out.

To receive the benefits of stimulating hair growth, you will need to perform some type of vigorous activity for a minimum of 20 to 60 minutes, three to four times a week. This vigorous activity must be executed non-stop between 60% and 80% of your Maximum Heart Rate (MHR).

What is your Maximum Heart Rate? It can be determined with a calculator and the following formula:

1. Subtract your current age from 220. This number is your MHR.

2. Multiply this number by 0.60. This will be 60% of your MHR.

3. Take the number you came up with in step 1. Multiply it by 0.80. This will be 80% of your MHR.

These numbers of 60% and 80% represent the range of your Target Heart Rate (THR). (**An important note:** Many high blood pressure medications work by lowering the heart rate, which would mean that your MHR and target rates may need to be lowered as well. If you are taking any blood pressure medications, contact your physician to find out how best to adjust these numbers.)

When engaging in exercise, you will need to keep track of your heart rate to make sure you are staying within the 60% to 80% THR range. This is commonly done by lightly pressing the index finger of the right hand over the artery just under the skin on the inside of the left wrist. The rate is easily determined by counting the beats for 15 seconds, then multiplying that number by a factor of 4. This will be your heart rate. (If you can't do the math in your head while working out, then try counting the beats for an entire minute.)

If you don't like the idea of measuring your pulse while working out, there is an alternative rule of thumb: If you can hold a conversation, you aren't working hard enough. If you can sing, you're not working hard enough either. If you are out of breath, or have to stop and catch your breath, you're definitely working too hard.

Whatever activity you chose, it is important to pace yourself. The goal is not to tire too quickly, but to maintain the level of effort so your body can receive the maximal benefits of your endeavor. When starting an exercise program, you should aim for the lower range of your Target Heart Rates, down around 60%. After several weeks, begin building up toward 75%, and then work toward the 80% goal only after six months.

Most people connect the idea of exercise with being miserable. The pictures of getting up at 5:30 to jog down a cold, foggy highway, or to pedal for a long, boring hour on a squeaky stationary bike immediately come to mind. Let's be honest here: These forms of exercise are not natural. (Of course, if you love to jog, or ride a stationary bike, by all means keep it up!) The point here is that the human body was designed for movement, and movement should be enjoyed as much as any other form of sensory stimulation. If jogging and riding stationary bikes seem like disagreeable and unpleasant forms of movement to you, then forget about them.

The human body was engineered for physical motion: walking, dancing, biking, playing games, and playing with children. These activities can get your circulation going, and your body will derive many benefits, but don't we really do those things for the fun of it? The point here is that moving your body should be as enjoyable as anything else you choose to do.

Start your program with very simple activities: Take a walk in the woods, or walk the neighborhood 30 minutes to an hour three times per week. Find a place to walk that is agreeable and pleasant for you. If you prefer, choose any of these other activities:

Bicycling	Racquetball
Canoeing	Swimming
Dancing	Tennis (singles)
Jumping rope	Volleyball

For people who can't engage in vigorous exercise, there is a lot of evidence that even moderately intense activities will bring about good health benefits. These activities can include:

Gardening	Tennis (doubles)
Golf	Touch football
House work	Walking for pleasure
Ping-Pong	Yard work

These are just a few ideas intended to get you thinking. Feel free to come up with your own. The key is to stay in vigorous motion for at least 20 to 60 minutes three to four times a week, and to make it fun.

Besides making it fun, the other key part to staying with an exercise program (indeed, even a hair growth and restoration program) is maintaining your motivation. Here are some key tips and tricks to keep you motivated:

Turn the volume down a few notches. Most people who start out on an exercise program often begin with a high degree of enthusiasm and impatience. This almost always leads to over-training, doing too much, too soon, and way too often. Rather than feeling healthier, the beginner winds up feeling really sore, worn out and sluggish—the motivation goes right out the window. Begin slowly and build the intensity over time.

If it ain't in the schedule book, it probably won't happen. Make appointments with yourself for exercise sessions. Be specific! Write down when it's going to happen, and where. (If you have a workout buddy, include the who as well.) Treat the appointment as you would any other. If you block out the time in advance and honor your word, you're more likely to keep that appointment. If you're a little weak on keeping your word with yourself, then find someone with whom you can communicate your schedule. After you work out, be sure to contact your committed listener so they can hold you to account as to whether or not you kept your word.

A workout in the morning is a great way to start the day. And, you get the whole matter out of the way right up front. You won't have to worry about whether or not you're really going to keep your workout appointment later on in the day, and you'll start the day knowing that you've already accomplished something positive. As well, morning workouts have a marvelously energizing effect that lasts for hours.

"Radio Saigon" is only one of the stations available on your dial. You know that voice in your head that criticizes incessantly, the one that says, "This is a waste of time! You're not getting any better, and your hair ain't growing back!" That one. It's impossible to shut it up, but you can drown it out by giving voice to the cheerleader inside you—literally, if need be. The cheerleader is the voice that cheers you on and is wild about your good points. This may sound a little weird, but give it a

try. You'll find it works very well. If you don't think you have a cheerleader, then make one up.

Keep going, even if you do just a little bit. Let's be realistic here. Sometimes you just don't feel like working out. That happens to everybody. Instead of giving up though, you should simply change your workout goals for the day to 15 or 10 minutes. The old adage that "Consistency breeds success" is as true today as when it was first uttered. A regular 10-minute workout is ultimately much more effective than doing an hour here and there.

Change is good. If things start feeling a bit stale, change the routine. If you go to a gym, go to the park once in while. If you normally run, try the Stair-Master or a rowing machine. Spice it up, and don't let it get boring.

Get a workout buddy. Or, schedule a few sessions with a personal trainer. Having the support of a partner can really inject new juice into a tired routine, and you will most likely learn a few things in the process. The contribution of a new voice should never be underrated.

Make it fun! Motivation starts to wane when the workout routine starts to become an obligation, something you have to do. Really look and see what you like to do, then do it. If it's dancing at home with the stereo blasting the latest #1 album on the pop charts, great! "Just do it," and have fun.

For a hair stimulation and restoration program, it is strongly recommended that you accumulate at least 30 minutes of physical activity every day in addition to your regular exercise program. What counts as physical activity? Anything that gets you moving. The trick is to be continually on the lookout for opportunities to move. Here are some ideas:

* Do a quick once-over in the garden to pull weeds.
* Pick your toddler up and lug the tyke around the house for five minutes.

- Bypass the elevators and escalators by taking the stairs.
- After lunch, take a 10-minute walk around the block and window shop.
- Play chase & fetch with the family dog.
- Get off the bus or train one stop early and walk the rest of the way.
- Instead of driving to the corner store to pick up a few items, walk.

This is going to require some discipline and vigilance, but, if you make it a game to reach 30 minutes every day, it can be a lot of fun.

As we've said before, obesity often means that your adrenal glands are not functioning properly and the vitamins, minerals and EFA's ingested with food and supplements simply get stored in the fat cells. Metabolically speaking, fat is nothing more than dead weight clogging up the system. One common misperception when starting any diet or exercise program is that the goal is to lose (or gain) weight. Yes, that's correct, but the bathroom scale is not the best tool for measuring whether or not you're overweight. Measuring the body fat content, or using the Body Mass Index (BMI) are methods that are far more accurate and useful in distinguishing if your body is functioning at peak levels. Recent federal guidelines state that a healthy BMI weight-to-height ratio should fall between 25 and 29.9. Anything outside those numbers is considered unhealthy, and requires action. You should see a professional trainer or your physician to determine your own BMI number.

While excess body fat is bothersome to your health, having too little is just as bad if not worse. A BMI number below 25 can wreak havoc with the immune system, cause fatigue, and interrupt the menstrual regularity and estrogen levels in women. It is also a cause of hair loss.

Whether your BMI number is below 25 or above 29.9, you should take action immediately. Start by seeing your physician, and perhaps a professional trainer for guidance. Every step counts in restoring your hair, and this one is no less important.

One final note: If you are over 40, have had any history of injury or illness, prescribed medications, problems with your bones, joints or muscles, are seriously obese or underweight, have experienced chest pains within the last month, have lost consciousness or fallen over due to dizziness, or have any other medical condition not mentioned here, you *must* consult your physician before beginning any exercise or weight-loss program.

17

Self-Hypnosis, Meditation & Visualization

Mind-Body Techniques for Manifesting Hair Growth

The past 30 years has seen a rapid expansion of scientific efforts to explore the mind's ability to act upon the body. The mind-body sciences (conventionally known as psychophysiology) recognize that the mind and body are so intrinsically interrelated that it is now regarded as irrational to consider any prescribed medical therapy as having an impact on just the mind or the body. Present day medical methodology now commonly employs the interdependent relationship of the mind and body, acknowledging the reciprocal influence of each to the other.

Clinical curiosity of the mind's role in the cause and development of illness and disease in the body has engendered an explosion of studies into the intricate interactions between the mind and the neurological, immune, and endocrine systems. Perhaps the most remarkable demonstration of this is the incontrovertible connection to the positive psychological state of cancer survivors as opposed to the despairing state of those who do not survive. And, we have all heard stories about the placebo response in some patients who miraculously recover from their ailments, only to find out later that their doctor has merely prescribed an innocuous sugar pill.

As we have shown over the previous chapters, the design of elements throughout the body (i.e., glands, hormones, proteins, vitamins, minerals, and EFA's) that produces a healthy head of hair is complex to say the least. With the ever-mounting credibility for the mind-body sciences, no hair growth and restoration program could be considered complete without exploring the options available. This chapter will inquire into a few of the most well-known and effective mind-body techniques, while presenting simple procedures and guidelines for implementing them into your personal program. Not only will these suggestions assist in balancing your body by promoting its proper functioning and lowering stress levels, but they will also serve to support and reinforce the lifestyle changes you are implementing from the guidance of the pages herein.

SELF-HYPNOSIS

Hypnosis has been a tool of healing for thousands of years. The early Greek temples often used hypnotic suggestion and the induction of trance states in therapeutic techniques. Variations of the Greek methods were used throughout the ancient world, often with a strong occult or mystical overtone flavoring the proceedings.

Franz Anton Mesmer is widely regarded as the father of modern hypnotism (hence, the term "mesmerize"). Mesmer introduced the 18th century world to a methodology called "magnetic healing" for treating a variety of psychological and psychophysiological disorders. His success at healing such maladies as hysterical blindness, paralysis, headaches, and joint pains did much to boost the credibility of hypnosis. The next big boost came from Freud, who initially proclaimed its remarkable effectiveness on patients who were suffering from hysteria. Later, he recanted his endorsement due to the troubling outpouring of powerful emotions from his patients, which by all accounts stemmed from his self-admitted ineptitude and lack of skill. Until the 1950's, hypnosis was relegated more to the parlor room than the research lab.

Today, hypnosis is used as a medical tool in the treatment of many common ailments, either independently or in concert with other treatments: pain management, reduction of bleeding in hemophiliacs, blood sugar stabilization in diabetics, controlling the severity of hay fever and asthma, as well as physiological reactions to allergens (such as certain foods), lowering blood pressure, curing warts, addictions to alcohol, nicotine and other drugs... The list goes on and on.

How does hypnosis, or self-hypnosis, work? It's actually quite simple, and there's nothing much mysterious or mystical to it. A subject enters a deeply relaxed state via an induction talk, or script. Once sufficiently relaxed, electrical activity in the brain slows from the fully conscious Beta State (13 to 40Hz) to the Alpha State (7 to 12Hz). It is at this point that the mind enters a condition in which the subconscious mind (the part of your brain running much of the show without you even realizing it) is rendered highly susceptible to suggestion.

Take note of that word "suggestion." A suggestion during hypnosis is the most effective way to spell out your goals and give instructions on how your subconscious mind can fulfill those goals. This is important, because studies have shown that the subconscious mind is limited to deductive logic in its operation. Deductive logic is the process of reasoning from the general down to the specific. For example, let's say you have known ten redheaded people in your life who were all hot tempered. A friend introduces you to someone else who is also redheaded. Deductive logic dictates that this new redhead must also be hot tempered. (Inductive logic is the opposite of deductive logic, which is to reason from the specific to the general; this is the basis of all scientific thought.)

This fact that the subconscious mind uses deductive reasoning is very important. Why? Because it means that a suggestion repeated often enough over a long enough period will eventually be accepted as true by the subconscious. This characteristic allows the process of hypnosis to work. As you begin applying the techniques of hypnosis, suggestions that are currently not true eventually become accepted by the subconscious as true and so are fulfilled.

This does not mean that silly impossibilities can be made true, such as growing an extra arm, dropping ten years off your age, or losing 15 pounds of weight over night. Trying to use suggestions that are impossible won't harm you physically, but will seriously damage all credibility for hypnosis with your subconscious. The subconscious will—by using its pattern of deductive reasoning—quickly come to believe that hypnosis is a waste of time.

Here are some basic rules to follow when formulating suggestions:

- *Be specific.* Describing specific outcomes is always more effective than generalities. (Emile Coué's famous auto-suggestion from the turn of the Twentieth Century is a good example of what to avoid: "Every day in every way, I am getting better and better.") Don't get so nitty-gritty with the details that you're actually explaining to the subconscious mind every single step from swallowing a B-Complex to the release of sebum in the follicles. Just stick with specific outcomes.

- *Be literal and avoid clichés.* Use care when choosing the wording of suggestions. Words like "cool" and "bitchin'" could be interpreted literally by the subconscious, leaving you with a reduced body temperature and a persistent fowl mood.

- *Be positive.* Keep the phrasing of your suggestions in the positive. If words like "don't, no, can't, won't," pop up in your phrases, try to rework them into a positive statement. NEGATIVE: "I no longer smoke cigarettes." POSITIVE: "Everyday my complete mastery over my former smoking habit increases."

- *Use "I," not "You." "I am," not "You are."* Remember that you are addressing a part of *yourself.* Your subconscious will think you are talking to someone else in the room if you use the second person imperative.

Now, you may be wondering if self-hypnosis is as effective as being hypnotized by someone who is professionally trained and licensed. The answer is, It depends. And, all hypnosis is really self-hypnosis. A licensed hypnotherapist merely acts as a guide for the patient or client. Naturally, for specific therapeutic treatments, a professional will almost certainly be more effective, but not necessarily by a lot. The sense of control that a person has during self-hypnosis more than counterbalances the advantages of utilizing a licensed hypnotist.

Do not be concerned about safety issues, as long as you stick to hypnotizing *yourself*. While under a self-induced trance, your mind still uses the same protective mechanisms as it does when you're fully conscious. In other words, you won't do anything during self-hypnosis that you wouldn't ordinarily do. (If you're thinking of a stage magician's show where you may have seen people doing some pretty strange things, don't worry too much about that. There is a psychological dynamic in a stage presentation where people under hypnosis experience a substantial pressure to do whatever they are told. Obviously, that dynamic will not be present during self-hypnosis.)

Some people worry about losing consciousness during self-hypnosis. This would only happen if you fall asleep. Otherwise, you may from time to time experience short lapses in memory, which appear to be moments of unconsciousness. This is nothing more serious than the ordinary occurrence of driving the car home from work, then getting out of the car and not being able to remember how you got home.

Other people worry about not being able to wake up. This is utterly impossible. The worst that can happen is that you would fall asleep. Think of it this way: During the induction process, you put every ounce of effort into getting *into and staying in* the trance state, rather than attempting to get *out* of it.

Almost everyone wonders if they can learn self-hypnosis and whether they are susceptible to being hypnotized. The answer is a resounding, Yes! Anyone with at least a roughly normal I.Q. and who is conscious once in a while can learn self-hypnosis and master it over time with practice. Susceptibility to the trance state only requires one thing: Willingness. If you're willing, then you can be hypnotized. Conversely, if you are not willing, then you *can't* be hypnotized.

Now, about the process of inducing a state of hypnosis, it is best to practice regularly—at least three times a week. For those suffering from alopecia or hair damage, it is *strongly* recommended that you schedule a session two times a day. Just as the chapter on exercise suggested, plan it out. *Put it in your schedule.* You will probably need about twenty minutes, depending on your level of susceptibility. Find a quiet room, close the door, unplug the phone, and sit or lie down comfortably. (If you think you might fall asleep, then don't lie down.) You may need some kind of white noise to block out the ambient sounds from outside the room. White noise can be either the static from an older FM radio tuned between stations, or an audiotape of the sound of waves rolling over the sand at the beach. Find something that is soothing and does a good job of masking the noise from all around you.

Below is an induction talk with suggestions for the areas of concern that are specific to those committed to hair growth stimulation and restoration. The areas covered are as follows: 1) The harmonious functioning of the body. 2) Reinforcing your behavior modifications in this program. 3) Reducing stress, while increasing confidence.

You will need to record this talk so you can use it to guide you into the Alpha State of a trance. While it is perfectly all right to record the script with your own voice, you may want to ask someone else to record it for you. This is because many people have an awkward reaction to hearing their own voice on tape, and it can be a distraction from the process. If you choose to have someone record it for you, remember to change all of the "I's" to "You's" and "My's" to "Your's." Whoever records this talk must use a positive, assured, and resonant tone of voice. The pace of the reading must be slow and measured. It takes some practice, and you may need to re-record a few times over. When you've got it right, you'll know it.

SELF-HYPNOSIS INDUCTION TALK

I am starting my self-hypnosis session now. From now until I say 'wake up' I will get more and more relaxed and focused within myself. With every breath, I will go deeper and deeper, more and more relaxed.

As I close my eyes, I take a deep breath and begin to drift downward, I feel a soothing pool of warm water covering my feet. My feet are becoming deeply relaxed, becoming limp and relaxed. As I begin to float downward into the pool, every part of my body covered by the warm water will become completely relaxed.

Now the water is moving up to my knees, relaxing every muscle and tendon. All tension is flowing out of my body from my knees down, leaving all the muscles limp and loose. I am getting more and more relaxed, more and more limp and loose. With every breath, I am going deeper and deeper...

Now I am drifting down further, and the warm, soothing water is moving slowly up to my waist. As it moves upward everything is becoming relaxed. As it reaches my waist I let go of all tension, allowing it to flow outward. All the muscles and tendons in my hips, lower abdomen, legs and feet are becoming relaxed, more and more relaxed.

All cares are flowing out of my mind. If a thought does intrude, I will just gently let it go away. I am thinking only of relaxing and letting go of all tension. All of my muscles are becoming more and more relaxed, and I am feeling pleasantly drowsy. I will not go to sleep, but I am feeling so carefree and relaxed, sinking further and further into myself with no cares or worries... Breathing deeply, going deeper and deeper...

Now the warm water is rising upward, moving slowly over my stomach, inching up over my chest, stopping at my shoulders. All of the muscles in my stomach and back are letting go, becoming totally... completely... relaxed... The muscles in my chest and arms are getting more and more limp. I could move if I really had to, but I am becoming so comfortably limp and relaxed I don't want to move. I am still and relaxed, drifting downward, ever deeper and deeper into an enjoyable, calming state of tranquility.

Now the warmth is slowly moving upward from my shoulders. The water level is remaining there, but the relaxation is delicately gliding upward. All muscles in my neck are becoming limp and flaccid... limp and loose. All cares and worries are floating away as I drift ever downward... with every breath going deeper... and deeper.

The soothing warmth is extending into my mouth, lips, and jaws. All tension flows outward and away... My tongue is limp, resting in my mouth with no need to be tense. Downward... Deeper and deeper... The warmth covers my cheeks and eyes, relaxing them... I could open my eyes if I wanted to, but it would be too much work. It would take too much effort to open my eyes. I am drifting pleasantly downward, becoming more and more relaxed.

The muscles in my forehead are becoming more and more relaxed... deeper and deeper, relaxing more and more with every breath. From the tips of my toes to the top of my head, I am becoming more and more relaxed, drifting downward... deeper and deeper...

Now, in my mind's eye, I see the pool of water opens out into a large, gently flowing river... The water is quietly moving through a lush, deep green forest... I am going to count down from twenty-five. As I count down I will begin to float with the river, drifting deeper, and deeper into the forest, pleasantly going deeper and deeper into a peaceful state of relaxation. I will get drowsy and deeply relaxed, but I will not actually go to sleep. I will simply drift deeper and deeper into my self-hypnotic state of deeply relaxed awareness. By the time I reach zero, I will be in a very pleasant, sleep-like state. I will still be able to direct my thoughts, and I could rouse myself immediately if I needed to, but unless I really need to, I will drift deeper and deeper into the relaxation.

Starting down now... twenty-five, I begin drifting along with the gentle flow of warm water... twenty-four... twenty-three... twenty-two... drifting deeper and deeper into the forest... twenty-one... twenty... feeling drowsier and drowsier, yet still awake... nineteen... eighteen... seventeen... floating gently downward with each count... sixteen... fifteen... fourteen... drifting, drowsy... thirteen... twelve... eleven... ten... more than half-way down, drifting deeper and deeper with each count... nine... eight... seven... six... five... feeling so relaxed... four... becoming more and more relaxed and drowsy... three... two... one... zero. Breathing pleasantly, slowly, drifting deeper and deeper with each breath.

As I continue to be deeply relaxed, and to become even more relaxed, I am thinking about my suggestions. I am resting, calm, and relaxed. In this state of absolute peace, I have an opening to my subconscious. This opening grows wide, more and more, and my suggestions are setting into my subconscious, taking root there. I will carry out these suggestions.

There is now an immediate increase in the life force energy in my scalp. The increased blood flow is bringing health and vitality to my scalp. I feel my scalp begin relaxing more and more, the entire scalp loose and relaxing. All the tiny nerves and muscles throughout my skull are deeply, thoroughly relaxed. The blood vessels are now becoming more elastic, releasing all tightness and constrictions, loosening into a perfect state of elasticity. The arteries and blood vessels are increasingly flexible and pliant. The blood flows freely through my body, carrying life-giving oxygen to my central nervous system, feeding my brain with strength and energy, while relaxing me deeper and deeper. The arteries and blood vessels in my brain and nerves are all completely relaxed. As the blood reaches my brain, it smoothly and properly feeds my body with the oxygen and nourishment it needs.

And, as I massage it consistently each and every day, this increased energy and vitality is flowing more evenly and more effortlessly. My increased blood flow to my scalp will move unhindered, giving me healthy and radiant hair.

I have a head full of hair. My hair is growing thicker, and I am losing less and less every day. All my hair is healthy and strong, firmly attached to my scalp. I am being complimented on my hair, which is thick, healthy, and getting longer.

The hair on my head and scalp is multiplying itself, as it should. And, the hair is growing faster and stronger with every passing day. It is actually growing thicker and multiplying itself. All the hair on my head and scalp is replacing itself as it should, multiplying itself, and going through its growth cycles as it should.

At present, the glands in my body are beginning to secrete correctly, with all my glands secreting correctly and fully, forming the flawless chemicalization throughout my body. Forming the flawless chemicalization throughout my body, my glands secrete the perfect mixture into my bloodstream, which is carried throughout all the parts of my body, including my brain, and follicles in my scalp.

My thyroid gland and the organs and systems in my body are balanced. And, they are secreting the proper chemicals to balance my body as they should. When the light from the sun touches my body, descending from the top of my head down to my toes, my nervous system, and all my organs, systems, and glands become balanced. All the cells of my body are suggestible and respond to my suggestions.

I find that I am confident in myself. I am confident, secure, and relaxed. I am confident in my own individuality, and I am confident in my ability to accomplish whatever I set out to accomplish. That includes the goals I am undertaking in restoring the health of my hair and stimulating its growth. I have full and complete confidence in myself to follow the program, and I have a calm, clear sense of absolute trust in myself. I have drive and vigor and ambition. I think in a positive manner. I am positive in my thinking. I am positive in my thinking. I have the utmost appreciation for myself, my gifts, and my skills.

I will do what I know is right, and I do know what is right. I let go of all sense of confusion. My mind is clear and free. I am thoroughly and utterly happy, enjoying life to the fullest. I thoroughly and fully enjoy life. I thoroughly and fully enjoy life.

I enjoy eating well and healthfully. I enjoy exercising, and feeling my body move and grow stronger. I enjoy my program for treating my hair, seeing my hair grow long, full, and healthy. Minute by minute, my hair is becoming thicker and thicker, fuller and fuller. It now glows with a beautiful shimmer. More and more of it springs from my scalp. Where there was little or no hair before, old roots regain their youthful power. I am delighted. My hair is once more becoming my crowning glory. I enjoy sharing my success with others.

I am from this moment forth at the standpoint of perfection. I have a perfect state of health. I am perfectly balanced physically and emotionally. I have a positive attitude, a positive frame of mind. My subconscious will immediately reject any negative thoughts that may try to enter my mind. My subconscious will immediately reject any negative thoughts that may try to enter my mind. I will stay positive, having complete confidence in myself.

Each and every day, I will become more and more confident in myself, and become more and more conscious of a perfect state of health, mentally, emotionally, and bodily.

Each and every day, I will become more and more confident in myself, and become more and more conscious of a perfect state of health, mentally, emotionally, and bodily.

I am the master of my own mind, and my mind is not the master of me. I am the master of my own mind, and my mind is not the master of me. Each and every time I hear these suggestions, they will be more and more reinforced within my mind. More and more reinforced within my mind.

All of the suggestions I have given myself will be effective because they are right for me, and it is good that I should achieve them. All of the directions I have given myself are good for me, and I will follow them.

Each time I practice self-hypnosis, I will become better and better at it. I will be able to relax deeper and deeper in less time with each practice.

Now, as I count to three, I am going to wake slowly, gradually, pleasantly. I will return to my normal, waking state, except for the suggested changes. Now, starting up... one... becoming more alert... two, getting ready to open my eyes... three, wake up.

Like it says at the end of the script, "each time I practice, I will become better and better at it." In rare cases, results are immediate with hypnosis. For most people though, it takes some time—plus, practice, practice, practice.

MEDITATION

While it doesn't take you "under" quite as deeply as a hypnotically induced trance state, meditation is a powerful alternative to hypnosis. Essentially, it is a self-directed practice for soothing the mind, and relaxing the body. Most meditation techniques used in the West have come from the religious practices of the East, chiefly India, China, and Japan, but it is common throughout all cultures of the world. Up until the mid-70's, meditation was considered strictly as a religious practice. However, a lot of medical studies since then have shown that meditation has a potent effect on reducing blood pressure, and the blood cortisol levels associated with stress, chronic pain, anxiety, serum cholesterol levels, and substance abuse, while increasing longevity, quality of life, intelligence-related measures, and emotional stability.

Once the mind relaxes into the meditative state, the brain waves have slowed to the Alpha State (7 to 12Hz). Many meditation methods employ visualization techniques for implementing changes in the mind and body, as opposed to the verbal suggestions of a hypnotic induction talk.

What follows is a suggested meditation journey, which can easily be modified according to your own preference. It is suggested that you do this at least three to five times a week to gain the maximum benefits. If you are choosing to include self-hypnosis into your routine with the recommended minimum of three sessions per week, then you might try meditating on two other days for at least 15 minutes each session.

Find a peaceful, quiet room away from distractions. Remember to unplug the phone, and use a white noise source to mask unwanted sounds that may disrupt your session. Sit or lie down in a comfortable position.

Close your eyes, and begin breathing deeply. Begin relaxing your body by starting with your toes, moving progressively up to the top of your head, focusing on relaxing every muscle, tendon and organ. Continue breathing deeply.

Once you've reached the last follicle and muscle on the top of your scalp, begin seeing yourself in your mind's eye moving or floating through a dark passageway. Continue moving through the passage, remembering to breathe deeply.

See the passageway open up into a beautiful, natural place—a place you've been before, someplace you've heard about, or it could be someplace you just make up. Whatever setting you create, it should be an environment where you feel completely protected and safe.

Take a few moments to look around, listening to the sounds, smelling the smells, feeling the feelings, tasting the tastes, as well as seeing what there is to see.

When you are ready, look up at the sky in your environment. Notice that there is a ball of pure, golden light descending from above. It pours its healing energy in through the top of your scalp, down through your brain, face, throat and neck, down through your shoulders, back and spine, down your arms, elbows, forearms, hands and fingers. The healing, golden energy pours through your bloodstream, opening the arteries, filling the lungs, heart, glands, stomach, genitals, and continues down the length of your legs, past the knees and on to the tips of your toes.

See this energy healing your body and improving its efficiency, instilling you with vitality, confidence, strength, inner calm, and peace… Whatever quality you desire.

Once you are complete with your healing, spend a few more minutes in your sacred place thanking it for being there. When you're ready, begin to move back out of your environment, moving back through the dark passageway.

Gradually become aware of your muscles, tendons and organs again, remembering where you are. When you feel ready, open your eyes and take a look around. Give yourself a good stretch, and stand up slowly (you might feel a bit lightheaded). Maintain an awareness of your inner sacred place and the golden healing energy flowing within you.

This is just one of the countless meditation techniques you can use. There are many excellent books and Internet resources available, should you wish to delve more deeply into the fascinating subject of meditation. It is a wonderful tool for improving health, and relieving stress—both of which are so critical to a hair growth and restoration program.

18
Reflexology & Other Things
Stimulating the Root From the Tips of Your Toes to the Top of Your Head

No one really understands why or how reflexology works. It is just does. Reflexology is an age-old, noninvasive mind-body therapy that is now prevalent in its use among medical professionals and alternative healers. Dating back to ancient Egypt and China, its benefits have been well documented over the centuries. It is based on the observation that certain reflex points on the hands and feet correspond to specific organs, structures, and systems of the body. These reflex points, when stimulated, bring about a response in their analogous regions. By using special pressure techniques on the feet and hands, any imbalances can be effectively treated to restore balance. The bioelectric flow of energy in the body, which is likewise manipulated in the practice of acupuncture, is aroused and strengthened by massaging these touch-points.

Reflexology is a valuable tool for hair growth and stimulation because it can be used to restore the delicate metabolic equilibrium of the blood and glandular systems feeding the scalp, while reducing stress, and promoting the overall health of your mind and body.

The routine below is very simple, and only takes a few minutes. For maximum benefit, you should *schedule* (there's that word again!) your reflexology routine at least five times a week. However, since it only takes a few minutes, you might consider doing it every day.

1. *Solar Plexus & Diaphragm Reflex Points* (14 X's each, left and right sides): *This exercise specifically helps to lower stress levels by stimulating the solar plexus to combat stress and anxiety.*

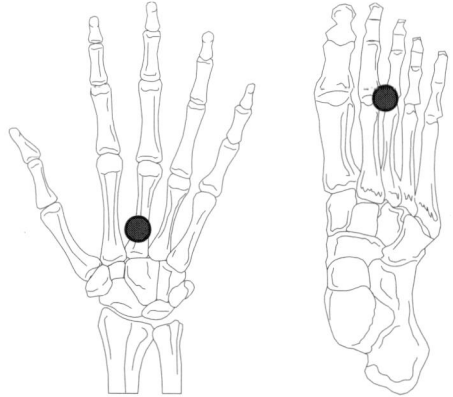

Solar Plexus & Diaphragm reflex points.

HANDS: The reflex point for the solar plexus and diaphragm are located on the palms of both hands, just below the pads of the middle finger. Place the thumb of one hand on the reflex point of the other hand and press firmly. Your hand may try to curl, so force it to keep straight since this will expose the reflex point for the best stimulation. Rotate your thumb over the pressure point. Repeat six more times, increasing the pressure with each repetition, and don't let up until you've completed seven reps. Switch hands and repeat.

FEET: This reflex point is centered just below the balls of both feet. Rotate the thumb just like you did with the hands, repeating seven times while maintaining and increasing pressure. Repeat on the other foot.

2. *Pituitary Gland Reflex Points* (14 X's each, left and right sides): *This stimulates the glands to secrete hormones regulating the functions of the other glands in the body.*

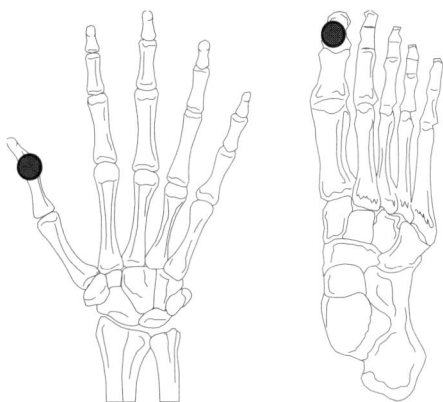

Pituitary reflex points.

HANDS: The pituitary gland reflex points are located in the center of the pads of the thumbs, and are pretty deeply positioned under the skin. Rest the thumbnail against the palm of the opposite hand, and press down into the pad of the thumb with your index finger. Press deeply, using a circular motion. Repeat seven times, increasing the pressure with each repetition. Switch thumbs and repeat.

FEET: This reflex is located in the center of the pad of the bid toe on each foot. Grasp the toe between your thumb and index finger, and press deeply into the pad with your thumb, moving it in a circular motion. Repeat six times, increasing the pressure with each repetition. Repeat on the other foot.

3. *Thyroid Gland Reflex Points* (14 X's each, left and right sides): *This stimulates the thyroid to improve the body's metabolic balance and heart rate.*

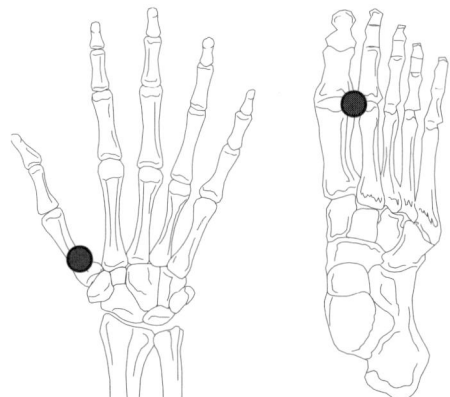

Thyroid reflex points.

HANDS: The thyroid gland reflex points are located on the palms near the base of the thumbs next to the crease between the thumbs and the index fingers, almost three-quarters of the way down toward the wrists. Apply a firm, rolling pressure against the points, starting light, then progressively increasing pressure with each repetition. Repeat seven times, then apply to the opposite point.

FEET: The thyroid point is located on the soles of the feet at the base of the big toe, just below the crease between the big and second toes. Apply your thumb in a firm rolling motion, gradually increasing the pressure over seven repetitions. Repeat on the opposite point.

4. *Lung Reflex Points* (14 X's each, left and right sides): *This stimulates the lungs to increase the oxygen level in the blood, nurturing the metabolic processes that feed the body (including the follicles of the scalp).*

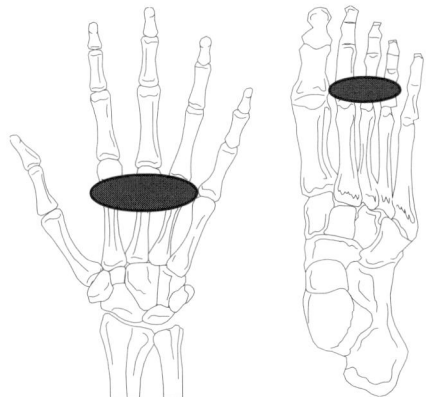

Lung reflex points.

HANDS: The right lung reflex point is located on the right hand, and the left lung reflex point on the left hand. The points are on the palms of the hands, under the pads at the base of the middle and ring fingers. Work the entire reflex area by applying the thumb of the opposite hand and working it in a circular, rolling motion. Press firmly, and increase the pressure over seven successive repetitions. Repeat on the opposite hand.

FEET: The right lung reflex point is located on the right foot, and the left lung reflex point is located on the left foot. The points are on the soles of the feet, under the pads at the base of the second, third, and fourth toes. Just like the hand points above, apply a thumb firmly and work it in a circular, rolling motion around the entire reflex area. Increase the pressure over seven successive repetitions, then repeat on the opposite foot.

5. *Heart Reflex Points* (7 X's each, left side only): *This stimulates the body's cardiovascular system, improving the pumping of blood.*

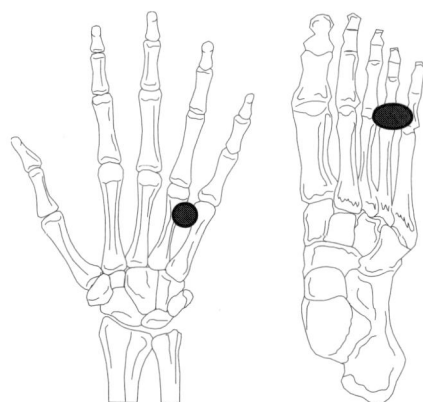

Heart reflex points.

HANDS: The heart reflex is located on the left hand, just below the pads of the ring and little fingers. Apply your thumb in a circular motion, gradually increasing the pressure over seven repetitions.

FEET: The heart reflex is located on the sole of the left foot, just below the ball of the foot under the fourth toe. Apply your thumb in a circular motion, gradually increasing the pressure over seven repetitions.

6. *Adrenal Gland Reflex Points* (14 X's each, left and right sides): *This stimulates the adrenals to secrete hormones that regulate the metabolism of fats, proteins, and carbohydrates, as well as promoting the health of the sebaceous glands and follicle ducts. Additionally, the adrenals enhance the heart tissue, as well as balancing sodium and potassium levels in the body.*

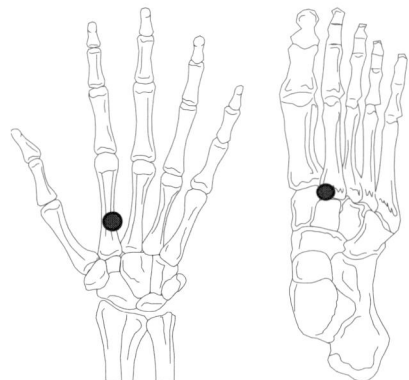

Adrenal gland reflex points.

HANDS: The adrenal reflex points can be found on both hands below your index fingers, just on the inside edge of the pad extending from your thumbs. Press firmly with the opposite thumb, hold for a moment, and then let up just a bit. Repeat by increasing the pressure gradually six more times, and then apply to the opposite hand.

FEET: Finding the adrenal reflex point is a bit more complicated. On the right foot, flex the toes with the sole facing you; this should reveal a slight ridge formed by the tendon extending from the ball of your foot to the heel. The reflex point is about halfway down, just to the right of the tendon. It's in the identical place just to the left of the tendon on the left foot. Press firmly with your thumb, hold for a moment, and then let up just a bit. Repeat by increasing the pressure gradually six more times, and then apply to the left foot.

7. *Kidney Reflex Points* (14 X's each, left and right sides): *This assists the kidneys to filter out toxins from the blood.*

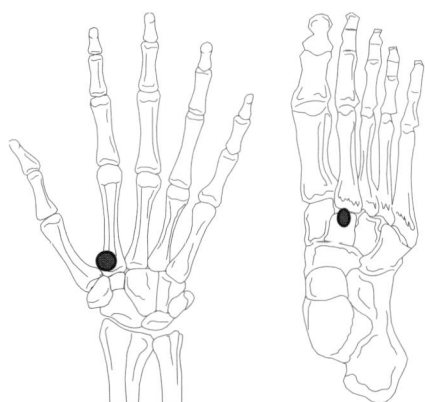

Kidney reflex points.

HANDS: The kidney reflex points are very close to the adrenal points on the palm of the hands, just inside the edge of the large pad at the base of the thumb. Press firmly on this area with the opposite thumb, hold for a moment, and then let up just a bit. Repeat by increasing the pressure gradually six more times, and then apply to the opposite hand.

FEET: Like the points on the palms, the kidney reflex points are very near the adrenal points on the soles of the feet. Flex your toes once again, and locate the soft, spongy area in the middle of the arch halfway between the balls of the feet and the heel. Press firmly with your thumb, hold for a moment, and then let up just a bit. Repeat by increasing the pressure gradually six more times, and then apply to the left foot.

8. *Liver Reflex Points (7 X's each, right side only): This stimulates the liver to store and release Vitamin A, an important factor in promoting the proper functioning of the sebaceous glands.*

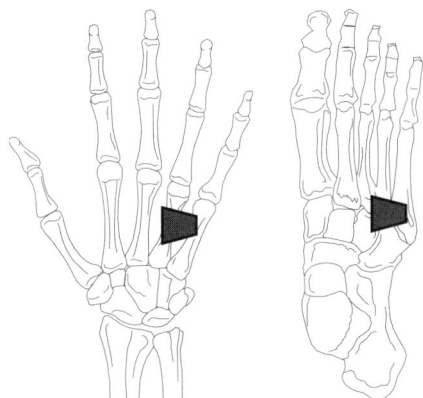

Liver reflex points.

HAND: The liver reflex point is an area found only on the right palm. Located about a third of the way below the fingers, extending horizontally from the little finger to the ring finger, and down to the top part of the pad of the palm and along the crease. Using your left hand, grasp the right hand and position your left thumb over the reflex area. Apply a firm, rolling pressure on the area, moving in a roughly circular motion. Increase the pressure gradually over six additional repetitions.

FEET: The liver reflex point is an area found only on the sole of the right foot. Located just under the balls of the foot, it extends midway between the base of the toes and the heel pad, with the inner edge extending downward from the crease between the third and fourth toes and over to the outer edge of the sole below the little toe. Position your thumb over the reflex area. Apply a firm, rolling pressure on the area, moving in a roughly circular motion. Increase the pressure gradually over six additional repetitions.

9. *Ovary & Testicle Reflex Points* (14 X's each, left and right sides): *This stimulates the reproductive glands to regulate the proper levels of hormonal secretions.*

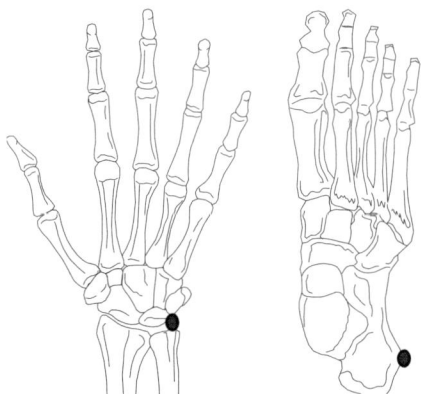

Ovary & Testicle reflex points.

HANDS: Since our bodies have two ovaries or testicles, the reflex points are found on both hands. Accordingly, the left reflex affects the left gland, and the right affects the right gland. The reflex points actually can be located on the wrist in the small hollow formed between the bone and the base of the palm. Gently, but firmly, press your index finger over the point, hold for a moment, and then relax slightly. Repeat six more times, gradually increasing the pressure with each repetition, then apply the same procedure on the opposite hand.

FEET: The reflex points on both feet can be found just above the middle of the hollows located below the outer ankles. Gently, but firmly, press your index finger over the point, hold for a moment, and then relax slightly. Repeat six more times, gradually increasing the pressure with each repetition, then apply the same procedure on the opposite ankle.

CHROMATHERAPY

Color has long been known to effect our moods, thinking processes, and even impact our health. Scientific research into color therapy, or chromatherapy, has demonstrated that certain colors can ease stress, fill you with energy, and assuage physical maladies and pain.

Color is visible radiation vibrating at subtly different wave-lengths. Cone-shaped photoreceptors in the eye's retina catch this energy, transmitting the information to the brain where it is interpreted as color. The retina contains three sets of cones, with each catching the light rays of red, blue, or green. We perceive different colors by combing information from these three colors.

When the color information is passed into the brain, it stimulates the pituitary and pineal glands, which in turn secrete hormones that produce a number of physiological processes. (This hormonal secretion is perhaps the key to understanding why some blind people can sense colors through touch, since the light and frequency information might somehow still be transmitted through the cones of the eyes to the brain.) Colors can be selected and placed in your environment to decrease stress, increase energy, or promote the health of the body. Attention should be paid to the colors in your home, office, and particularly with the clothes you wear. Below are listed several colors and their known effects. It is vital to adjust your environment when attempting to restore your hair and promote growth.

Blue is relaxing, and has a deeply calming effect. Blue lowers blood pressure, the heart rate, and respiration. If you are suffering from stress-related alopecia, you might consider painting your walls a tone of blue, or at least the room where you relax and meditate in. While meditating, or practicing self-hypnosis, include a visualization of the color blue.

Green has a similar, soothing affect to blue, and has a markedly relaxing effect on the body and mind. People who are depressed or anxious, should consider redecorating with green, and adapting their wardrobes to this color. Green also helps nervous disorders, exhaustion, heart problems, and cancer.

Violet is also soothing, and is known for suppressing the appetite, aiding kidney problems and migraines, and for *relieving scalp conditions*.

Shades of *pink* are often used in hospitals, prisons, and drug treatment centers because it relaxes the muscles and soothes the body. It tends to have a tranquilizing effect on aggressive and violent people. It is also known to assist people suffering from anxiety and withdrawal symptoms. Pink also engenders feelings of peace and romance, so it works well in the bedroom.

Red stimulates, excites, and invigorates the body, increasing the heart rate, brain activity, and respiration. This is the color of energy, vitality and passion, and is good for anemia, bladder infections, skin, and scalp problems. You might consider using red wherever you exercise.

Yellow is stimulating, but is a bit milder than red. It has an energizing effect, lifting the spirits, alleviating depression, and is known to treat muscle cramps, hypoglycemia, gallstones, and overactive thyroids. It is also regarded as the color of memory, which is why most note pads are printed on yellow paper; it has a positive effect on the brain's memory center.

AROMATHERAPY

Aromatherapy has grown increasingly widespread over the past couple of decades, as its effects on the human mind and body have become commonly accepted. Much like the interaction of light waves with the cones stimulating the pituitary and pineal glands, the sensory information transmitted through the nose also interacts with the brain. The olfactory system is comprised of hair-like receptors in the mucous membranes lining the roof of the nasal cavity. Nerve fibers connect the receptors and pass through tiny holes in the nasal cavity, forming two structures called the olfactory bulbs where the sensory data is collected. Smells then travel from these bulbs along nerve fibers into the olfactory center of the brain, which in turn fire off the consequent hormonal secretions.

While the evidence for aromatherapy's healing effects on the body remains largely empirical, there does appear to be a direct correlation to our well-being and the smells we smell. (Indeed, much of how the olfactory system interacts with the brain is still not understood.) Aromatherapy is not something new. Practiced throughout the ages, it has been used as a curative to combat many ailments. The veritable explosion in sales of incense and essential oils over the past few years would indicate that the public has caught on and doesn't need to wait for definitive proof.

Nor should you.

There are lots of options available for aromatherapy, such as incense, candles, dried herbs, and potpourri. They smell really wonderful and do have healing properties, but by far the most effective form is an essential oil. Essential oils are exceedingly aromatic, containing much of the healing properties of the herbs and plants used in the oil extraction process. Make sure that the oils you purchase are 100% pure and natural, preferably chemotyped essential oils from your herbal supplier or health food store.

Below is a chart of herbs and plants that can be purchased as an essential oil and used for your program. Feel free to experiment by selecting several different oils and mixing a few drops of each in a lamp diffuser, or in a bit of water in an oil warmer (which are widely available at drug stores, or from your herbal supplier). If you like, you can also carry a small vial around with you, and take a few moments to inhale the scent of the oils throughout the day. Keep in mind that a few drops of these oils can also be added to your shampoos, conditioners, and rinses as well. (First, do a test on a small patch of skin to make sure there is no allergic reaction.)

Essential Oils	Healing Properties
Basil:	Used for relieving mental fatigue and stress.
Bergamot:	Used to alleviate sebum buildup in the skin and scalp, eczema, psoriasis, and for treating depression due to its general uplifting quality.
Birch:	Promotes hair growth, and is beneficial for relief of muscle pain and arthritic discomfort.
Cedarwood:	Prevents hair loss, eczema, psoriasis, acne, and reduces stress & tension.
Chamomile:	Treats skin conditions, such as dermatitis, boils, acne, rashes, and eczema. It is also used for general health of the hair, and treats stress and its related complications such as insomnia, and migraine headaches.
Clary Sage:	Balances hormone secretions, and promotes good circulation.
Clove:	Treats thyroid imbalances, and reduces stress.
Cypress:	Much like Fenugreek, this cleanses the circulatory and lymphatic systems of mucous, allowing for improved metabolic saturation of nutrients.
Davana:	Stimulates the endocrine system, and balances hormonal secretions.
Fennel:	Stimulates the cardiovascular and respiratory systems feeding the scalp.
Fir:	Supports the body in fighting a great number of ailments, and is stimulating to the circulatory system.
Frankincense:	Used as an antidepressant, and is stimulating for the mind; also reduces stress.
Geranium:	Balances hormonal secretions, and is known to regenerate tissues and nerves. Promotes healthy functioning of the pancreas and liver, and is also regarded for its anti-stress and anxiety reducing properties.
Ginger:	Promotes proper digestion, and is a stimulant for circulation.
Grapefruit:	Promotes proper digestion, and assists in stimulation of hair growth.
Helicrysum:	Improves circulatory functions, improves skin conditions, and is known to assist in reducing stress.
Hyssop:	Stimulates the respiratory system, and expels mucous and other toxins.
Jasmine:	Reduces stress, and relieves depression.
Juniper:	Cleanses the system, discharging toxins; treats eczema; promotes improved kidney function, and reduces stress.

Essential Oils	Healing Properties
Lemon:	Promotes health of the skin and scalp, while improving the lymphatic glandular system; and elevates a sense of well-being.
Lemon Grass:	Purifies the system, and promotes functioning of the digestive tract. Lowers stress, and acts as a sedative.
Myrrh:	Beneficial for skin & scalp conditions, including eczema. It also works to support the prostate gland, while stabilizing thyroid secretions.
Myrtle:	Balances hormonal secretions of the thyroid system and ovaries.
Nutmeg:	Stimulates the adrenal glands for increased energy, while elevating the mood and increasing a general sense of well-being. Supports circulation and proper digestion, and relieves stress.
Orange:	Promotes a sense of peace and tranquillity.
Oregano:	Works very much like Thyme, but is more potent; helps to stimulate the immune system, balances the metabolism, fortifying the vital centers of the body.
Patchouli:	Is known to be a general tonic, and a stimulant for the digestive system. It also works to relieve stress, and promotes a general sense of well-being.
Pepper (Black):	Stimulates the endocrine system, and increases energy. Also increases cellular oxygenation.
Rosemary:	Heals skin & scalp conditions, including eczema and psoriasis, balances sebum production in the follicles, and prevents hair loss; supports the immune and endocrine systems; also reduces stress and mental fatigue.
Sage:	Heals skin & scalp conditions, including eczema and psoriasis, balances sebum production in the follicles, and prevents hair loss. Stimulates the metabolism, and reduces stress and mental fatigue.
Sandalwood:	Works very much like Frankincense, and is used as an antidepressant, and is stimulating for mind; also reduces stress. Increases oxygen flow to the pituitary and pineal glands.
Spearmint:	Supports the respiratory, nervous, and glandular systems. Elevates the mood, and promotes a general sense of well-being. Also good for increasing the metabolism, which reduces body fat.
Spruce:	Much like Spearmint, it supports the respiratory, nervous, and glandular systems. Elevates the mood, and promotes a general sense of well-being.
Tangerine:	Good for reducing stress, nervousness, and anxiety; acts as a sedative, and produces a sense of calm.

Essential Oils	Healing Properties
Thyme:	Supports the immunological systems, and acts as an anti-microbial cleanser. It is also known to soothe the nervous system, reducing stress and promoting a general sense of well-being.
Wild Tansy:	Improves the immune system, and elevates the mood, producing a positive attitude and general sense of well-being.

19

Putting It All Together, The Daily Checklist

Your Day-by-Day Regimen for Optimal Hair Growth

Now that you have all the information that you need to know, let's put it together. Below is a reference framework of all the steps described in Chapters 5 through 18 you should include in your daily, weekly and monthly regimen to promote the optimal growth of your hair, and restore your scalp to its peak vitality:

Chapter 5—The Program: Remove the hair care products from your bathroom.

Chapter 6—The Big Picture: Begin by taking *photographs* of your hair and scalp from the front, left and right profiles, the back of the head, and the top of your scalp. This should be scheduled and repeated every 120 days.

Chapter 7—Shampoos: *You must shampoo every day without fail.* According to the needs of your particular hair type, use the *Essential, Willow & Birch, Energizing Citrus,* or *Aloe Vera Moisturizing Formulas* with a selection of the herbs of your choice.

Chapter 8—Conditioners & Rinses:
Conditioners: Use the *Essential Conditioning Formula* with an herbal infusion of your choice, and as determined by your hair type and needs, three to four times a week.

Select one of the *Hair Pack* formulas and use once a week.

Use a *Scalp Pack Formula* once a month with an herbal infusion of your choice, and as determined by your hair type and needs. People with dry or oily hair should repeat this step three to four times a week for the first four weeks of the program, then two times a week for the second four weeks, and thereafter once a week for maintenance.

20

In Conclusion...

A Few Last Words

Many clients who walk through the doors of *Riquette International* come with a deep sense of anguish, fear, and frustration over the condition of their hair. Their stories are fraught with a great deal of pain and anger, and are often profound in their shame and loss of hope. Our task in repairing the health of our client's hair is never just about the scalp. It also requires compassion, understanding, and a heartfelt commitment to recuperating their lost sense of self-esteem. Our work is only complete when joy, vitality, and pride have been healed.

Trust. Love. Integrity. Peace. These are the four elements we work with and strive to instill in our clients. The men, women, and children who come to us must learn to trust that there is hope, and that they have not reached the end of the line so to speak. They must have compassion for their selves by releasing the fear and anger; this is an act of self-love. Most clients look in the mirror, see only their hair loss and damage, and believe that they are flawed. The mirror doesn't reveal the truth that they are every bit as lovable as the day they were born. We teach them to look deeper, beyond the brutal reality of their condition, and see the essence of their spirit. As it says in the ancient Vedic scriptures of the *Bhagavad-Gita*, "Life is love, and love is life. What keeps the body together but love?"

While trust and love are the foundation of the program, the promise of restored vitality and health can only be fulfilled by following each step with absolute integrity, the third element. A rigorous adherence to the coaching and guidelines set forth in these pages naturally augments the first two elements of trust and love as the desired results inevitably begin to show up.

These three factors of trust, love, and integrity are wholly integral and interdependent toward the accomplishment of their recovery. With accomplishment comes the final element, peace.

The transformation of your body, and specifically of the hair on your head, requires a feat of courage and faith. This can be more than a little frightening for some people who suffer from hair loss or damage. Until this instant, you may only have experienced discouragement and doubt.

Just consider for one brief minute that the only thing that may be blocking you from recovering your crown of glory is just that: discouragement and doubt. These feelings, which are totally valid, and perhaps quite justified, may in fact be the very things that keep you from achieving your goals. Think back on how often you've heard of a remedy for your particular malady, then tried it and failed, or didn't give it a shot at all. There may just be a seed of doubt taking root on some level in your mind. Take a look and see if it isn't there...

And then, consider that true courage comes from the willingness to face your fears and doubts head-on by acknowledging them, and acting anyway. Perhaps Euripides defined it best almost 2,500 years ago when he said that courage is "to bear unflinchingly what heaven sends."

The advice conveyed within these pages has, hopefully, given you enough information to reason with your fears, surmount them, and commit to the program. Results always begin with a commitment. Nothing was ever achieved in human history without this critical step. Ask yourself now, Are you willing to set aside your fears, trepidation, skepticism, or past failures and misfires and make a commitment anyway? If the answer is Yes, then read the contract below. Type it out, or write it on a piece of parchment or cardstock. Feel free to modify it, if you'd like. Sign it and date it, then post it somewhere where you can see it (i.e., your office at home, or your bathroom). Whenever you begin to doubt yourself, come back and visit it for a dose of encouragement.

CONTRACT FOR COURAGE AND FAITH

I, _____, understand that I am committing myself to an act of courage and faith by undertaking *Riquette's Total Hair Growth Program* for one year. I commit myself to faithfully fulfilling the requirements of the program from (*today's date*) to (*one year from today*) as outlined in The Program Summary in Chapter 19.

I, _____, further acknowledge and understand that this program requires dedication, perseverance, and the courage to keep going to produce the results I desire. I, _____, pledge to take excellent care of my mind, body, and spirit—plenty of rest, exercise, nutrition, play, and spiritual practice—for the entire fifty-two weeks of this program.

_____
(signature)

_____
(date)

As Mark Twain once said, "Courage is resistance to fear, mastery of fear—not absence of fear." Congratulations! In spite of your feelings, you have set yourself on the brave road to recovery, on the path to a transformation of your life.

A word of prudence, though: Commitment comes and goes as surely as your emotions swell and dip. It is necessary to acknowledge this, too. After all, you are human, so remember to also have compassion for yourself. Embrace your humanity, and be aware of the instants when your commitment wanes. That is when you want to refer back to your contract.

Now that you are committed, there is only one thing left: Action, the sister element to commitment in producing results. The best advice here is to simply take it one day at a time. Of course you want to schedule your meditations and exercise ahead of time, but you want to focus only on the here and now—the present. For that is all that really matters, isn't it? What you are doing in the present moment, on this present day. Putting your attention on all the activities you have scheduled tomorrow, next week, or next month will only tend to overwhelm you. Similarly, placing your thoughts on what you did yesterday, or how you didn't do so well last week, doesn't serve you either. Nothing will, and nothing *can*, serve you more than simply being mindful of today. After all, isn't the past already here and gone? Isn't the future already on its way? Has it ever needed your assistance in getting here?

Plan ahead to stay with the program, but give yourself the gracious gift of taking it in single, manageable one-day segments. Gradually, over time, you will see remarkable results. The fears, doubts, skepticism, and cynicism will fade with the recovery of your crown of glory. Ever-increasing excitement, confidence, and gratification will displace those old, familiar feelings. That is perhaps the greatest benefit of this program, one that has been hardly touched upon in these pages. By healing your hair loss or damage, you are also healing your inner self, reconnecting with your potential for joy, aliveness, and self-expression.

Trust. Love. Integrity. Peace.

Hair Growth Success Stories: Photo Gallery

As you've learned, hair damage and loss can have a wide variety of causes, and even multiple causes in the same person. But by taking a holistic, "total-person" approach, it is possible to overcome hair loss, grow new hair, and keep it for life.

I have treated thousands of individuals who have successfully re-grown hair. For this section, I have selected photographs of success stories from people suffering from a variety of conditions. It's very likely that you will identify with one of the cases represented in this gallery.

The "before" and "after" photos speak for themselves. I've included this section not only as an indication of the variety of hair-loss problems, but also to serve as inspiration to you. If you're the "before" now, you can be the "after" simply by following Riquette's Total Hair Growth Program.

Photo Gallery

Male Pattern Baldness in a Woman

We all have "male" and "female" hormones. Sometimes it is possible that a woman's male hormones can overpower her female hormones in a way that affects her hair growth or loss. In this woman's case this condition resulted in Male Pattern Baldness. By using Riquette's approach, she was able to re-balance her hormones and re-grow her hair.

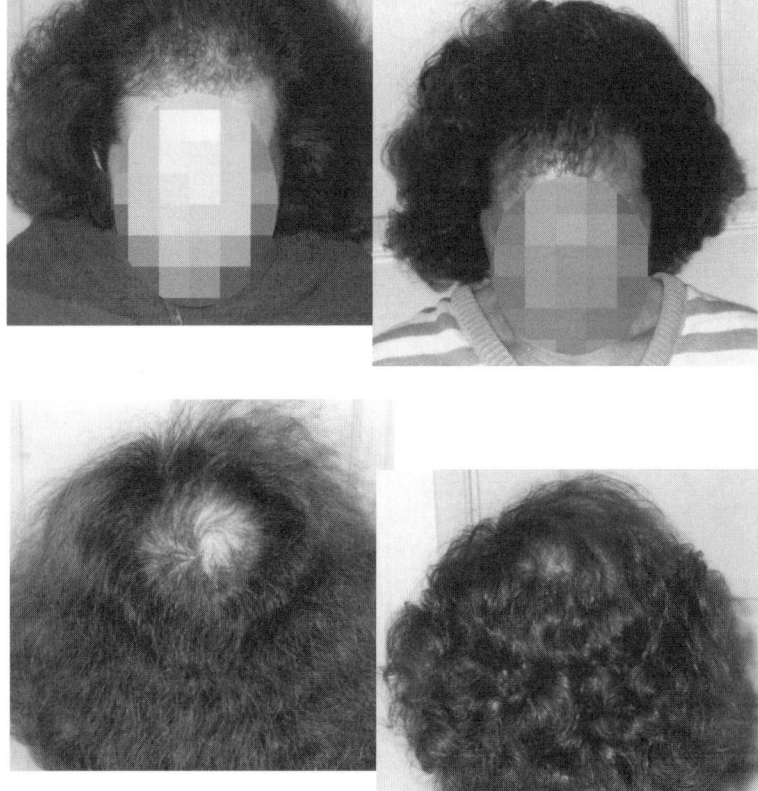

Traction Alopecia from Wearing Tight Caps

Many people wear hats and caps for fashion, work, or to hide their hair loss. Such headwear restricts blood circulation, cuts off oxygen and traps excess oil on the scalp. This construction worker wore a hard hat daily and a cap nightly, resulting in hair loss and keeping new hair from generating. By following Riquette's Program, he was able to rejuvenate his scalp and re-grow his hair.

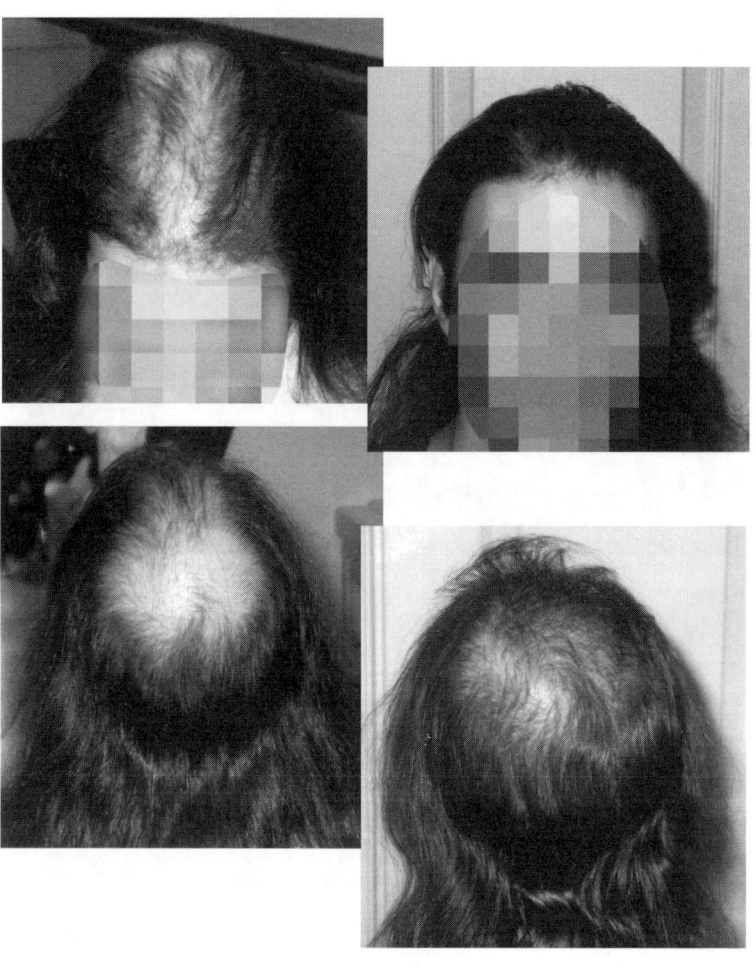

Drugs, alcohol and medication

The stress of a high achieving lifestyle combined with drugs, alcohol and medication can result in excessive hair loss as in this man's case. By following Riquette's method for the whole-body approach, the health of his body, mind and hair was vibrantly and naturally restored.

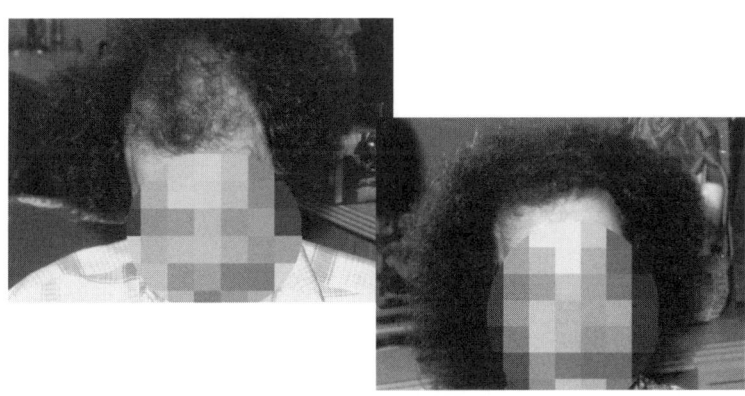

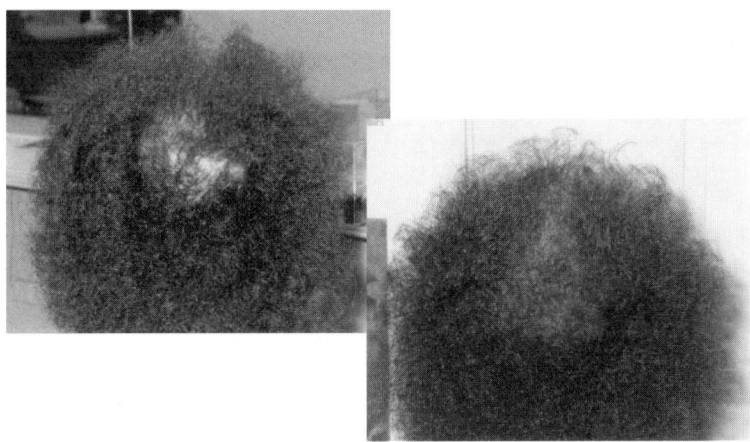

Stress Related Hair Loss

This gentleman was in a very chaotic business called show biz. Following the Program, eating well, using the stimulators he regained most of his hair back and it's still growing.

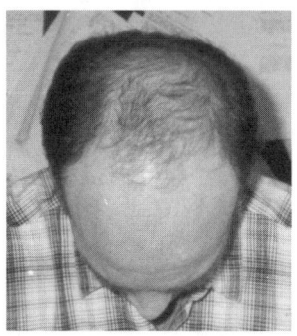 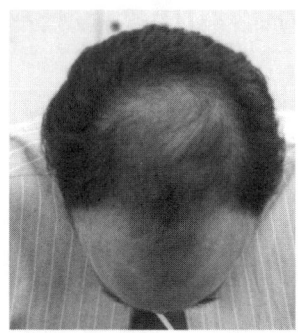

Disruptive lifestyles

Many of us who have a hectic schedule, which includes travel, do not believe that we can maintain a commitment to proper hair care. Hotel shampoos, fast food and hair dryers can result in making a baldness predisposition worse. Despite a heavy workload and travel schedule, by following the whole-body approach, this man in his 30s was able to restore his hair.

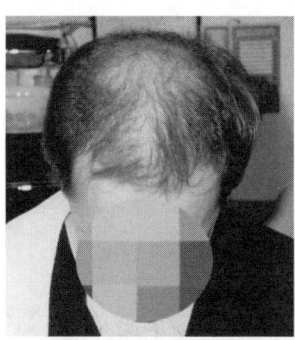 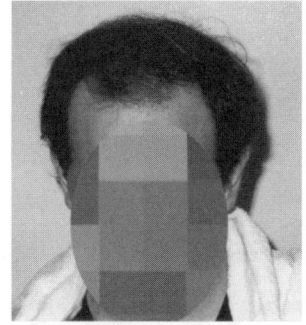

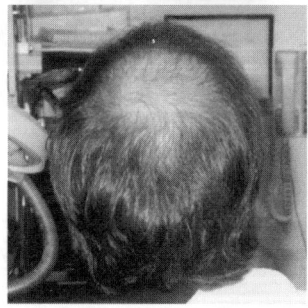 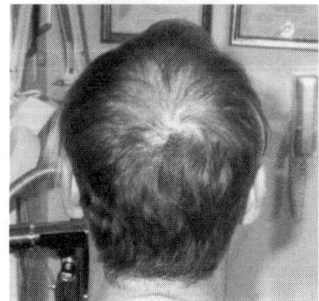

Chronic Chemical Treatment Can Cause Hair Loss

Harsh chemicals used for hair straighteners in this African American man penetrated and damaged the root, which began to cause his hair loss in clumps. After suitable treatment following Riquette's advice, his hair returned to a normal growth pattern.

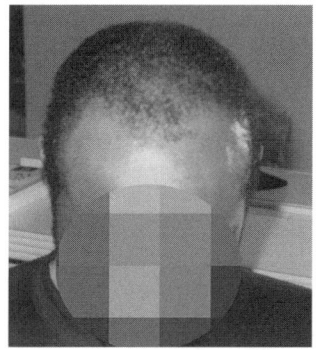 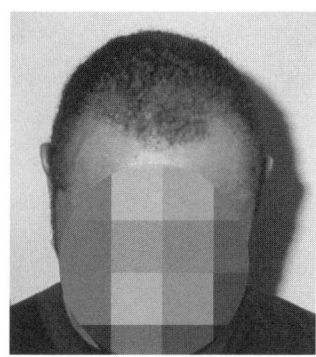

Oily Thinning Male Hair

Male pattern baldness is not the only common result of heredity and environment. Thinning hair often results from oily hair roots. The process was well under way in this young man. The natural whole-body approach was successful in renewing his hair growth.

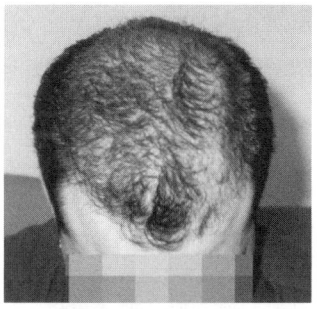 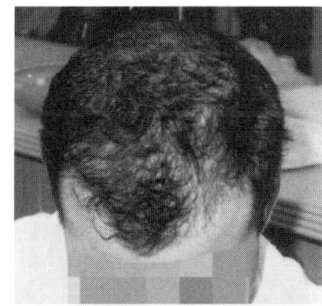

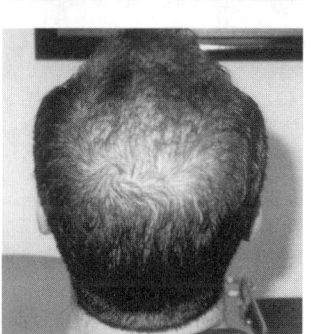 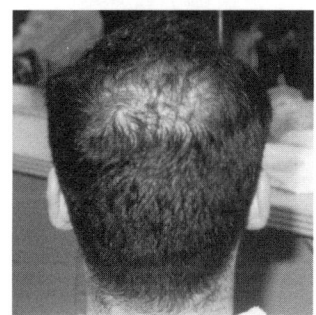

Curly, oily hair

Curly hair can be deceptive. Often people think that they need to use conditioners to tame their hair, when in fact it contributes to clogging and suffocating the pores as in this young man's case. Following Riquette's whole-body approach the scalp released the accumulation of unwanted trapped cells and his scalp began to breathe and generate new healthy hairs.

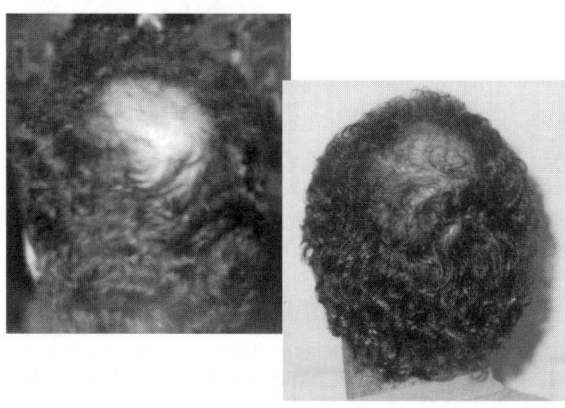

Unmanageable Thin, fine and oily hair

Commercial hair products promise, but often don't deliver, they can make matters worse. This woman chemically treated her fine oily hair and used hair products that contributed to hair weakening. Riquette's natural whole-body approach restored a healthy balance and gave her a healthy head of hair.

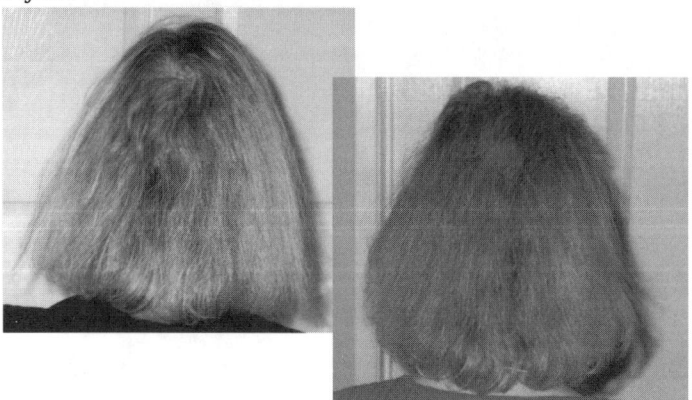

Exercising or Heavy Exerting Can Cause Hair Loss

Many people exercise their body but forget to properly care for their scalp and hair. Heavy exertion causes the combination of excess perspiration and natural oils to build up on the scalp and clog the pores. This person used only water to cleanse his hair after working out, which left the oils and resulted in a shiny, waxy build-up. By following Riquette's Program, he was able to dislodge the oil from his pores and re-grow his hair.

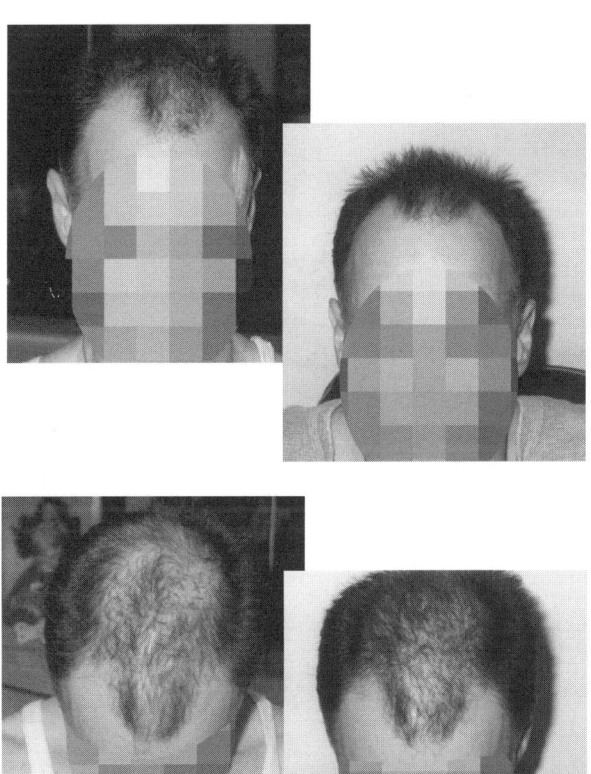

Birth control, pregnancy and menopause

Hormonal changes from birth control, pregnancy and menopause can attribute to hair loss. This woman was experiencing hair loss due to menopause. Women can avoid this devastating problem and learn through Riquette's approach how to rebalance their system so proper hair growth can return.

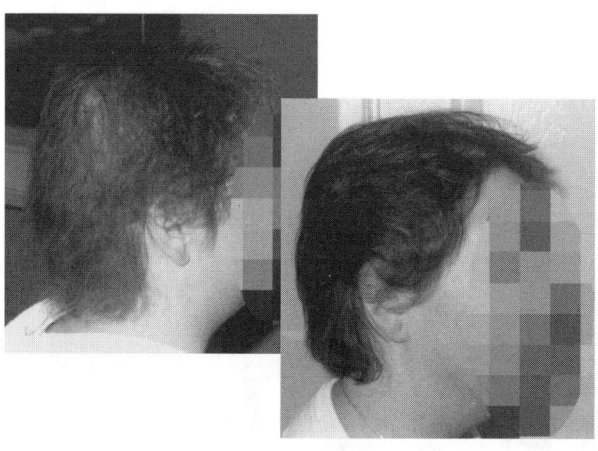

Anorexia, Bulimia and Yo-Yo Dieting

In a quest to improve appearance by weight loss, many people neglect proper nutrition. This woman tried numerous diets to lose weight. However, hair loss resulted. By following Riquette's whole-body approach, she achieved her desired results in areas of body, mind and hair.

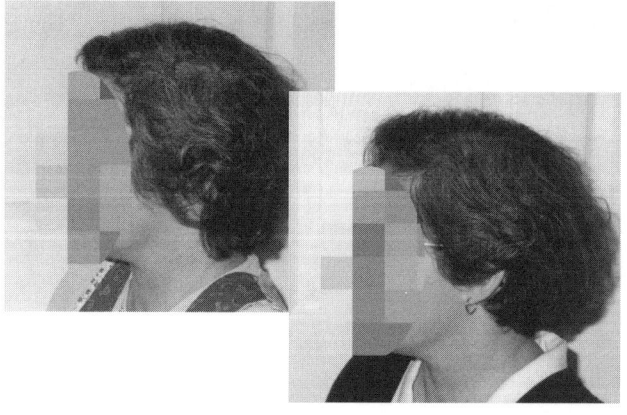

Wigs, hairpieces, hair extensions and chemicals

This Aftrican American Woman was wearing wigs and hats to hide her Alopecia condition. A few months after following the Program of using no chemicals, eating well, massaging her scalp, washing her hair without applying any grease on her scalp, learning to meditate and using the self-hypnosis suggestions, she is finally free of wigs and hats.

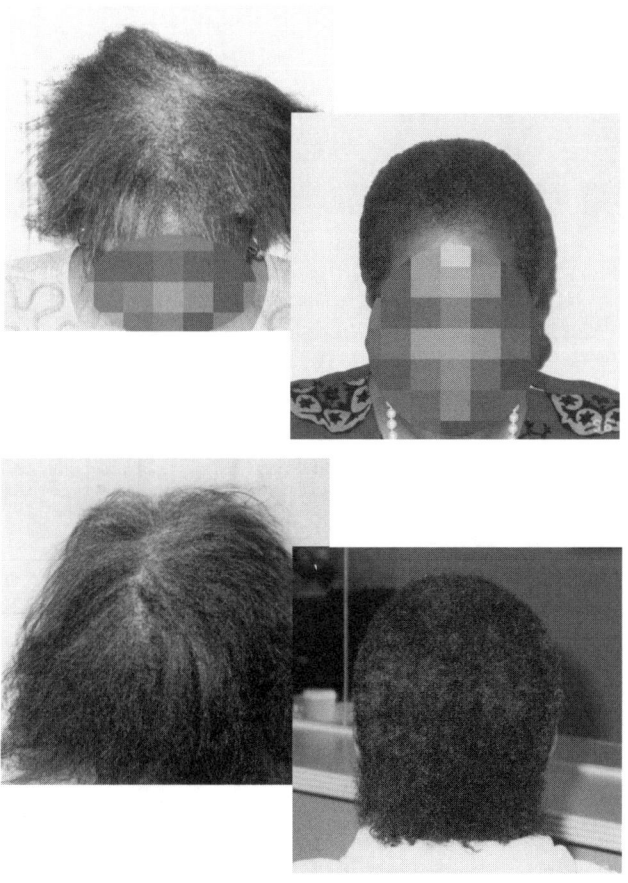

Emotional Trauma

Life events can be stressful, however, some can be so serious that they result in lasting psychological disruption and harm. Physical symptoms, which may include hair loss, frequently accompany such trauma. This female subject was abandoned as a child and began to experience hair loss as a young adult. By following Riquette's natural, whole-body approach and recognizing the connection between her former trauma and her hair loss, she was able to overcome her condition and experience normal hair growth.

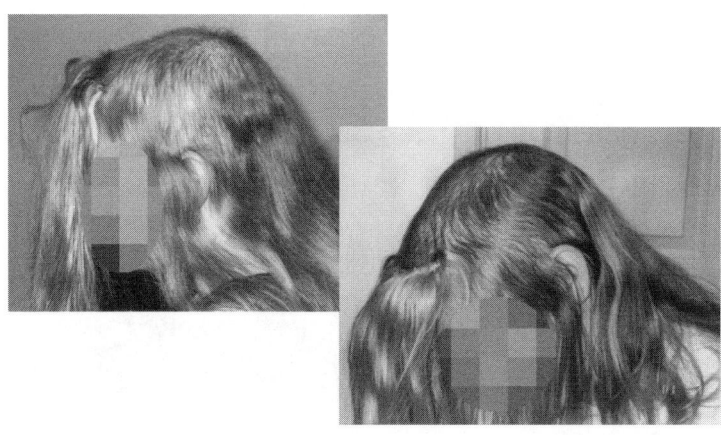

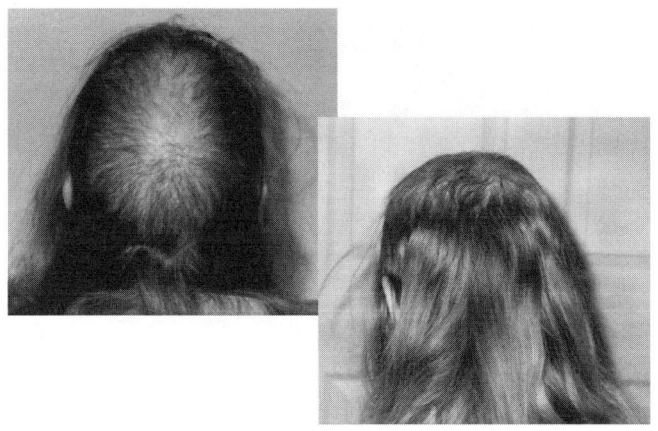

Peer and academic pressure

Many young people are so concerned with getting ahead in school that they deprive themselves of what their bodies need to maintain proper growth. This college freshman was experiencing sleep loss, poor nutrition and stress resulting in accelerated hair loss. By following Riquette's Program, he experienced a turnaround mentally and physically, with a dramatic improvement in his hair growth.

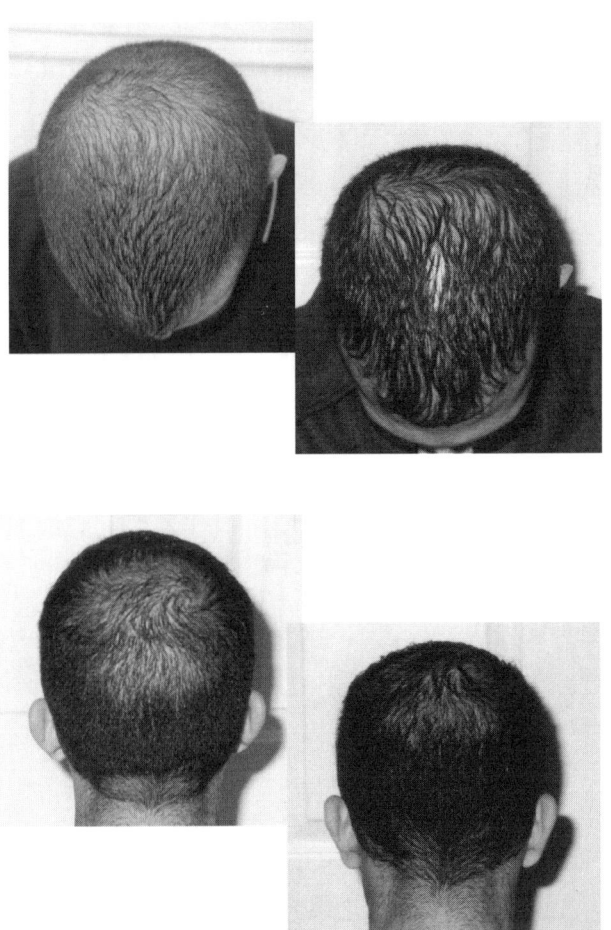

Reversing "destiny"

Many people believe that parental hereditary baldness is their fate, however, this is not so. Following all of Riquette's whole-body approach, including adoption of a proper mental attitude, yielded results in one month that began to reverse the severe balding in this 25 year old man.

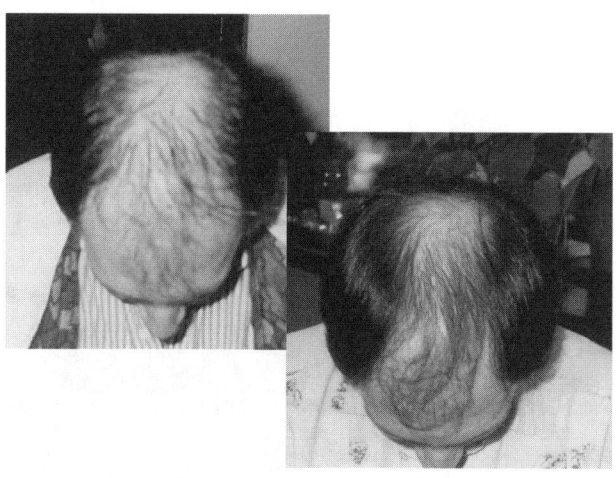

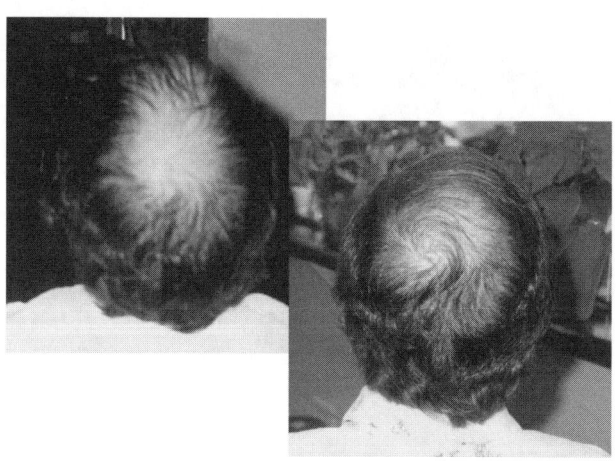

You can reverse aging baldness

No matter how old you are you can reverse Male pattern Baldness. This gentleman is 71 years of age and his life wish was to have a head full of hair. Following Riquette's Program, his life long wish was accomplished.

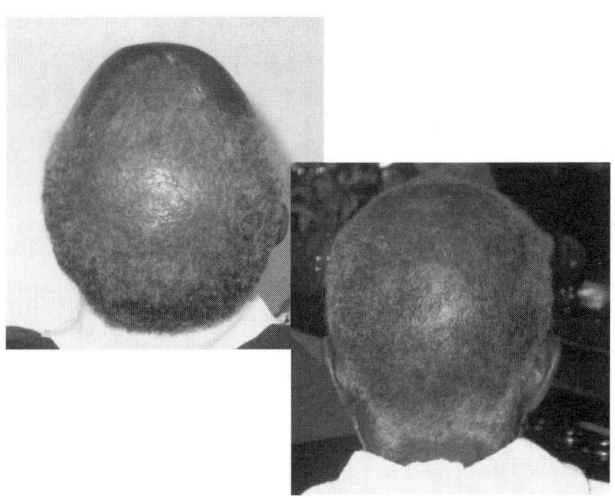

Index

About the Author

My motto in life is that everyone is beautiful. My goal is to enhance that beauty in the most natural way possible"
~ Riquette Hofstein

According to beauty expert Riquette Hofstein, your daily beauty regimen does not have to be expensive, time consuming, or perceived as mere self-indulgence. "Everyone deserves to look and feel their best, and by using a little common sense along with the right natural ingredients, anyone can achieve very expensive-looking results in just minutes a day, for a fraction of the cost."

The author of *International Beauty Secrets*, and the best seller, *Grow Hair in 12 Weeks*, as well as the **originator** of "kitchen cosmetics," (the heretofore unknown process of making one's own fresh moisturizers, mud packs, and scalp stimulators from items found in one's own pantry), Riquette has earned an international reputation for her unique approach to natural beauty.

Long before back-to-nature and environmental causes were fashionable, Riquette was appearing on national television and radio demonstrating her art of "kitchen cosmetics," offering audiences a healthful, inexpensive alternative to over-the-counter beauty products using fruits, vegetables and other natural ingredients.

Her unique blends include a special "vegetable soup" for the hair, a mixture to rid the scalp of excessive wax build-up to promote hair growth; a homemade Retin-A, using only natural ingredients; and a salad you can eat and wear, because according to Riquette, many of the ingredients in your salad bowl are the same components found in expensive cosmetics and beauty products.

In accordance with her philosophy of natural beauty and her concern for the environment, Riquette also has her own line of beauty and hair products, made out of natural ingredients. All her formulas are environmentally safe, contain no chemicals, and are not tested on animals.

Born in Cairo to French parents and raised in Paris, Riquette received her beauty training in the classic European tradition under the masters of makeup, hairstyling, and skin care. She holds eight degrees and certificates in skin, and hair care from colleges and institutes around the world including the prestigious Schwarzkopf Institute of Hair Research in Munich. She is professionally licensed in 14 European countries, North America, Australia, and the Far East.

Riquette has made numerous television and radio appearances including *CBS This Morning*, *Live With Regis and Kathie Lee*, *The Merv Griffin Show*, *CNN*, *A.M. Los Angeles*, and *Late Night with David Letterman*. She was an instant success with Letterman's audience, mixing up toothpaste as a scalp tonic, and using kitty litter and eggs for a facial mask amid ever more exotic creations from the average household pantry. Her witty banter played off Letterman's wry humor, and she was consequently booked on an almost unprecedented 15 shows in the past several years.

In addition to lecturing, writing, and making television and radio appearances, Riquette does private beauty consultations at her Beverly Hills clinic, Riquette International, where her star-studded clientele includes celebrities such as Ally Sheedy, Joan Van Ark, David Hasselhoff, Elizabeth McGovern, Morgan Fairchild, and comedian Dennis Wolfberg, as well as studio executives, doctors and attorneys:

Riquette has been described as a beauty queen who's never won a title, but in the business of making people beautiful, she is a winner with a royal touch.

Seminars & Workshops
How to Grow Hair in 12 Weeks!
with Riquette Hofstein

Located in **Beverly Hills, California**, we are a full-service alternative health and beauty clinic dedicated to making people healthy and beautiful from the inside out!

Riquette Hofstein will teach you proven techniques to stop hair loss and stimulate hair growth — using inexpensive ingredients you can find in your own kitchen and without expensive drugs or surgical implants.

You will discover:

◆ Why 99% of hair loss, thinning and damage is caused by one thing!

◆ Inexpensive natural stimulants that actually reverse the process of hair loss for only pennies a day!

◆ How nutrition and exercise affect hair growth!

◆ How to wash, rinse and brush your hair to protect and preserve it!

◆ And so much more!

Riquette Hofstein has been featured on dozens of TV shows, including David Letterman (15 times)! The author of Grow Hair in 12 Weeks and International Beauty Secrets, her clients include Hollywood celebrities and athletic sports super stars.

For locations and times, please visit our web site:

www.Riquette.com

Coaching & Consultations

Riquette is currently accepting new clients for private one-on-one and corporate/group coaching sessions!

Coaching sessions cover a broad range of topics and criteria:

◆ Stress Management

◆ Life Strategy Planning

◆ Corporate Training

Fees vary according to the nature of the coaching session or workshop.

For more information or to schedule an appointment, call our office at 800-747-8388. All appointments are strictly confidential.

RIQUETTE INTERNATIONAL
Riquette Hofstein, President
269 S. Beverly Drive, Suite 200
Beverly Hills, CA 90212
Phone: 310-551-5253
Fax: 310-551-5254
Internet: www.Riquette.com
E-Mail: Riquette@Riquette.com

TO ORDER MORE COPIES...

Internet Orders ✆: www.Riquette.com

E-Mail 🖳: Riquette@Riquette.com

Phone ☎: (310) 551-5253

Fax Orders 🖷: (310) 551-5254

Regular Postal Mail Orders ✉:

RIQUETTE INTERNATIONAL
269 S. Beverly Drive, Suite 200
Beverly Hills, CA 90212

For postal orders, mail this order form with your payment to the above address. Do not send cash and no COD's. Thank you!

Name: _____

Address: _____

_____

City: _____ State: _____ ZIP: _____

Country: _____

Phone Number: _____

E-Mail Address: _____

Credit Card: ❏ Visa ❏ Master Card ❏ AMEX

Credit Card#: _____

Expiration Date: _____

Billing Address:

City: _____ State: _____ ZIP: _____

Country: _____

PRICE: $24.95 plus Shipping & Handling! (U.S. Dollars)

Shipping & Handling: $5.50 for the first book PLUS $2.50 for each additional book ordered. (U.S. Dollars)

International Orders: Add $5.00 (U.S. Dollars) Per Book Ordered.
CA Residents: Add 8.25% Sales Tax (Calculate before S&H)

TOTAL $_____ENCLOSED!

Prices and availability subject to change without notice. Please allow one to three weeks for delivery. Thank you for your order!